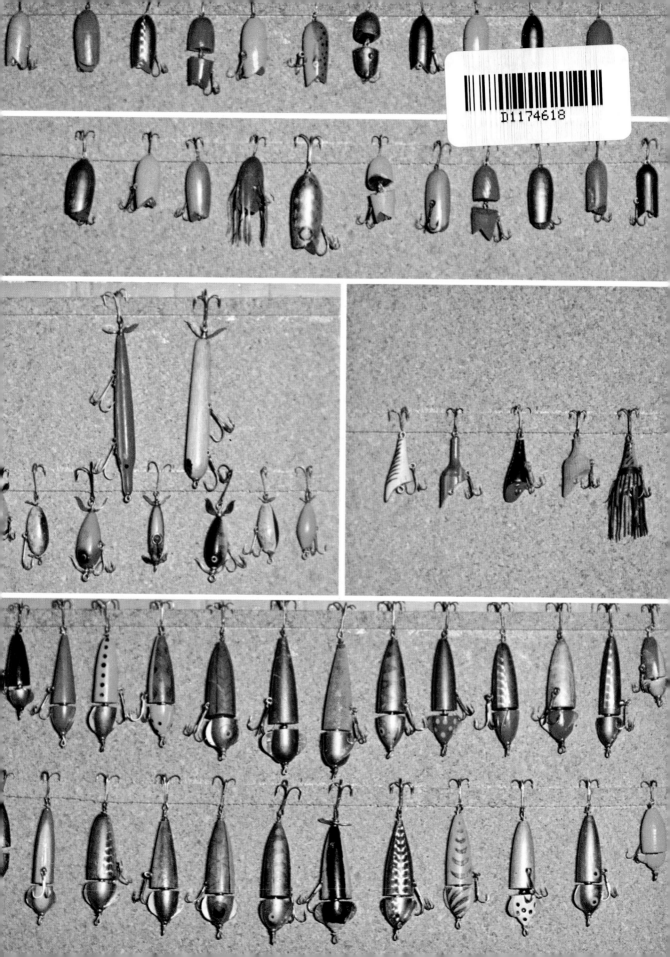

Charles K. Fox

the book of
LURES

ACKNOWLEDGEMENT

John C. Rex and the author have spent many happy times together both working and fishing. There were times when we cast our lures along lake shorelines for bass and muskies, and there were times when, with fly rod in hand, we cast our flies for trout or salmon of the little rivers or the large ones. We were together when John caught his first muskie and his first Atlantic salmon. When fishing by wading, I employ one of his excellent homemade chest kits which he presented to me. It is with appreciation that I look upon the fellowship of those times, and it is with gratitude that I thank him for his offer, his indulgence and his skill in photographing the lures pictured within this book.

Chapters 13 and 14 are reprinted from *Advanced Bait Casting*, G. P. Putnam's Sons, 1951; the Appendix is reprinted from *Fly Fisherman* Magazine.

ISBN: 0-88395-019-7
Library of Congress catalog card number: 73-79753
Manufactured in the United States of America

Designed by Joan Stoliar

overleaf: TOP
This muskie, taken early in the century from Lake LeBoeuf, Pennsylvania, appears to be as long as they come—a 5-footer.
BOTTOM:
One eerie November morn, as the sun burned off the dense fog, this muskie viciously struck a bobbing and weaving homemade Sick Sucker cast by Charlie Fox. The tiger was then returned to strike another day. Photos by Bob Lenig

To the memory of my Dad, who was with me when I caught my first bass and my first muskie, events which took place in 1921 as we fished out of Bobcaygeon in Pigeon and Sturgeon Lakes of the Kawartha chain in Ontario.

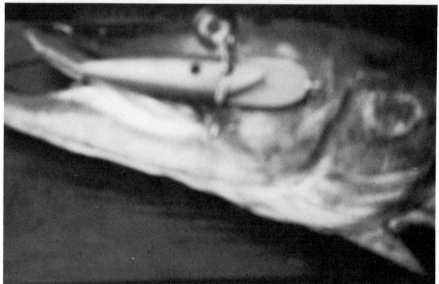

TOP: *The record Pennsylvania smallmouth was taken on a River Runt Spoon, November, 1943, from Kinkora on the Susquehanna River by the late Nip Boyer.*

BOTTOM: *Muskie and sick sucker, a great combination.*

Contents

Northern pike caught many years ago by author on a Pikie Minnow. Photograph taken by his fishing companion, Bob Klotz.

Introduction

My trail has led through fifty seasons, and with numerous companions it has brought me to many waters. During its course I've learned many things, but nothing has become more evident to me than the facts that the American sport of lure casting for game fish is a tremendous phenomenon, and the quarry we seek, the basses and the pikes, are great strikers and great fighters. Many people are so geared to lure casting for game fish and have enjoyed it to such an extent that the quality of their lives has been much enhanced.

I am grateful to have been a child at the time of World War I, because immediately after "the war to make the world safe for democracy" lure casting for bass developed and spread like wildfire. This form of angling quickly captivated the fancy of a tremendous army of anglers, as well as the interest of the tackle manufacturers and the editors of the outdoors publications. I got into it in the 1920s and was carried along with its development.

By the 20s, smallmouth and largemouth bass, neither of which were native to the East, had been introduced into the waters I knew and had become well established, the former in the streams and the latter in the lakes.

A parade of lures hit the show cases, and as soon as a new item of equipment was placed on the market, I bought and tested it. I was just in time to grow up with the two main phases of angling in America—lure fishing for bass with the bait-casting rod and multiplying reel, and dry-fly fishing with the fly rod for rising trout. By the late 20s I had become a dedicated disciple of both. Fly fishing for trout and lure fishing for bass and muskies were placed on the same high plane then, and that remains my attitude to this day.

I made trips to the Kawartha Lake Region of Ontario for bass and muskies and to the Blue Sea–Gatineau River section of Quebec for bass and pike. My home waters were, and still are, the Susquehanna-Juniata river systems of southern Pennsylvania.

Game fish are great school masters. After the new angler has learned the basics from these indispensable teachers, he can obtain his higher learning from the conversation and writings of other anglers. To a certain type of mind, it is both satisfying·and rewarding to progress from the primary grades right on through graduate school. It is to such anglers that this book is directed. In a sense, reading becomes a part of angling.

A game fish is self-reliant and alert. He is suspicious and crafty. He is a creature of moods and fancies. He is strong, fast, and determined. If he were any easier to catch, there would be none left. If he were more difficult to take, there could be but little catching. The balance is perfect. The path of the lure caster is strewn with fascinating problems, many of which he can solve. It is not my purpose to dwell at length on the various senses of fish, but let it be stated that the most successful anglers are those who attribute keen senses and great shyness to the game fish they seek.

One must know fish,‘ fishing methods, and fishing tackle. The challenge of sport fishing has four facets—locating the quarry, determining its moods, choosing the type of lure to be used, and delivering the goods. It must be recognized, though, that what is a productive situation for one angler may be unproductive for another.

Sport fishing involves some strange paradoxes. It is certainly among the strangest of all sports and is sometimes beyond the comprehension of the nonangler. We set forth to catch fish, but we do not want to catch them too easily. We like to catch large ones, but we do not want them all to be the same size. We do not like the experience of a fish getting away, but we do not want to land all that we hook. We are after fish, but we do not want to kill every fish we catch. Obviously the necessary requirements in a successful fishing formula are some success combined with a certain degree of failure, and both in conjunction with considerable uncertainty.

In our fishing, everything is relative. What might be a giant fish in one environment may be a pygmy in another, and vice versa. The more hazardous the cast, the greater the challenge. The more complicated the landing, the more cherished the catch. There is only one measure for this sort of thing, and that is in terms of personal satisfaction.

Many unrelated factors are involved. Ten percent of the fishermen catch more than seventy-five percent of the fish taken. Every cast is an adventure, and one cast can be the making of a day or a trip. Lure fishing and lure casting are not necessarily the same. Each stream or lake section has its own peculiarities. What a fish wants and what we hope he will want may be very different. Loosing a fish is not a failure; it is a partial success. The fish that get away often teach us more than the ones we catch. And so it goes. With age, the regular angler becomes a better observer, a keener analyst, and a finer practitioner.

I am a purist in that I use only artificial lures, but not because I do not believe in the use of bait (that's the way I started), but rather because the use of the artificial gives me more pleasure and satisfaction.

There may be no unanimity of opinion when we come to consider the problem of which lure to use at a given time in a given place. But come along with me in the hope and expectation that we will arrive at some accurate conclusions and that as a result you will enjoy some good fishing, both in and out of the pages of this book.

Surface Lures

Floating Underwater Wobblers

Sinking Underwater Wobblers

Sinking Propeller Lures

Weighted Hair, and Spinner

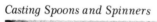
Casting Spoons and Spinners

Plastic Worms

Jigs

Classification of Lures

We can't give all our time to casting; some time must go to studying. Is there any phase of angling that is more interesting, more confounding, and more worthy of study than the matter of what one should attach to the business end of the line? Such considerations start with the various categories of lures and end with decisions as to how the various types fit into the angler's scheme of things. Involved with all of this are such factors as the angler's habits and locality, as well as the temperature, time of day, time of year, and water and weather conditions. The angler who comes up with the best answers catches the most fish; thus knowledge is power, and power is a gratifying thing to possess.

First of all, it is basic that a casting lure have pulling power. We do not want to handicap ourselves by attempting to cast lures that are too light for our tackle. Then, too, a lure must be lifelike in appearance and action, and it cannot be overpowering to the degree that it frightens the fish or makes them suspicious.

In my judgment, we should primarily attempt to attract rather than deceive. Wild colors, mechanical devices, odd forms, and crazy actions are all a part of our American game of lure fishing. It is an American game because lure invention and evolution center around large- and smallmouth bass, and these great fish are native only to certain midwestern states and Canadian provinces of our continent. Their redistribution has been one of the great conservation achievements.

We now live in a time when low unit cost, a five-to-one markup and other considerations of mass production have overwhelmed handwork and craftsmanship in lure-making. In the days of the pioneer lure-makers, painstaking methods were still possible. In the beginning there were many intricate lures, whereas today the commercial artificial is fairly simple. Unfortunately, because of the economic considerations, life has expired for some of the best-designed and most effective lures.

How about the angler who desires to be a finished artist, an upper classman in the school of angling? He can make for himself special lures that are better bets for certain anticipated situations. A new do-it-yourself lure-making cult is developing to take a place beside that of the fly-tiers, and the suppliers of fly-tying materials have added lure-making ingredients to their stocks. I make it a point to write about great lures past and present and to show clear pictures of the antiques, so the hobbyist can supplement the available supply of lures with facsimiles of old creations.

The following are the eight basic types of lures that I propose to study.

1. Surface Lures
2. Floating Underwater Wobblers
3. Sinking Underwater Wobblers
4. Sinking Propeller Lures
5. Weighted Hair, Feather-Skirt, and Spinner Combinations
6. Casting Spoons and Spinner Blades
7. Plastic Worms
8. Jigs

The "bass plug" underwent its period of greatest development in the two decades after World War I. Once it was accepted that bass and the pikes could be induced to strike a lifelike artificial lure, and once the equipment was readily available to cast such a lure, imagination and ingenuity ran rampant, as did the various claims for commercial lures.

Surface Lures

*See picture section
beginning on page 19.*

A man named Ans Decker made and sold a white surface bait with metal ears that made the head spin and splash water on the retrieve. He advertised the Decker Bait as the best lure made anytime, anywhere. Another angler, "Smiling Bill" Jamison, who also had a commercial lure, challenged Decker to a bass-catching contest, an invitation that was promptly accepted. The Decker Bait had three hooks, with hook points out. The Jamison Coaxer was equipped with a single hook, with the hook point up.

When the contestants, with a following that included news-hawks, arrived at the lake Jamison had chosen, Decker was fortunate that he did not suffer heart failure. Before them was a lakeful of lily pads so closely spaced that there was nothing that could be termed open water. Obviously the Decker Bait with its multiple-hook arrangement did not have a chance, whereas the Coaxer was designed to be a pad jumper. To make matters worse for Decker, he was equipped with a flexible rod and light line to facilitate casting, whereas Jamison was geared to railroad the fish out of the pads and up to the boat with sturdy tackle. Jamison caught some bass and thereby won by default. Later Pflueger manufactured the Decker creation calling it the Globe Lure.

During this time Jim Heddon had on the market a fat cigar-shaped surface bait with a sloping metal collar that rippled the water. He named his lure the Dowagiac, after his home town.

Reprinted editorially from Field & Stream *1902.*

Later his company came to be known as James Heddon's Sons, and in the 1940s they proudly advertised the Dowagiac as "being old enough to vote." The South Bend Bait Company produced a competing lure, worked on a lathe to have a symmetrical collar. They called it the Woodpecker Plug. The Creek Chub Bait Company specialized in a lure with a concave face that was appropriately named the Plunker. Both Creek Club and Heddon produced floating propeller plugs, calling them Crippled Minnow and Injured Minnow respectively.

Just before the start of World War II a quartet of lure designers conceived and produced a series of surface baits that were different in looks and principle from any that had come before.

Jim Donley outdid himself when he produced the Jersey Wow in the days when New Jersey had the three-hook-point law. The Wow had two metal arms protruding frontward that would paddle and gurgle and rock the lure. Later Heddon purchased the rights for it and placed it on the market as the Crazy Crawler. Donley's second lure was named after a funny paper character of the day, Barney Google. It featured a very large propeller on the blunt front end of a chunky plug. This was unique in that with stop-and-start rod-tip manipulation it would swing about and swap ends.

A man by the name of Hallek manufactured an artificial frog with movable legs. South Bend sold a similar one called the Vacuum Bait, which was shaped like a shield, the front of which, with the three points forward, would throw a spray. Creek Club produced a big bug with two single hooks, points up, to be fished in the pads.

In the bobby-socks era Fred Arbogast perfected and manufactured his great gurgler, the Jitterbug, which under the loving care of Dick Kotis is to this day a popular favorite. Its companion piece, the Hula Popper, combines a rubber skirt and a popper face.

George Phillips founded the Phillips Tackle Company, which produced the Crippled Killer, a smaller version of the old Injured Minnow. Heddon came out with the Tiny Torpedo, a floater with a blunt nose and a prop on the back end. More recently Rebel has produced a classly little humpback prop lure, the Spinback, which features their beautiful finishes.

Gone now are the Decker Bait, the Globe Lure, the Jamison Coaxer, the Woodpecker Plug, the Vacuum Bait, the Creek Chub Bug, the Barney Google and Heddon's Dowagiac.

All game fish become more surface minded when the water is warm and clear. If bass and muskies will not feed by daytime during a heat wave, they will feed on top at night. Thus, night fishing becomes the hot-weather safety valve for the ardent lure caster.

The magnetism of the surface lure is obvious. The strike of a game fish is a great thing to feel, but it is at its best when it is seen and heard as well as felt. This combination is electrifying. In spite of the fact that the surface lure has limitations—mainly in cold and broken water—it has its big innings in calm, warm water.

One bright August night I saved a special place for a fishing dessert. Scuttlebutt had it that a fine big ledge pocket in Conodoguinet Creek harbored a big bass that defied anglers. Ever so carefully I waded into casting position on the shallow ledge, attempting to prevent waves of information from giving the alarm to a naturally suspicious fish. At the end of the monofilament there dangled a tricky little surface lure known as the Baby Popper, a short-lived Shakespeare product of the 1940s. The Baby Popper was special in that at rest it floated in a vertical position. Rod-tip manipulation brought it level, and as it did so, the big concave face produced a *plip* sound often accompanied by a bursting bubble the size of a tennis ball. It was not meant to represent any specific creature of nature; it simply resembled something alive. The most effective way to retrieve it was to make haste slowly with a jerk-and-wait movement. Overeagerness disrupts calm water, and that scares bass. Over the years this ¼-ounce lure has been a great one for me, especially on river smallmouths. I still have about a half dozen of them.

The little lure had no more than hit the water when I gave it some lifelike action. I then permitted it to settle down as the rings widened. After the pause I gave it a series of jerks. The sudden noise of the explosion out there was nerve-racking. It is amazing how unexpected the expected can be.

Automatically I struck back, and the throbbing rod signified a heavy fish. The bass made a power run, then jumped. I was so excited that my breathing came in gulps. After two more jumps and about ten minutes of give and take I got that fish in the net head first and lifted him out of the stream. That is the sort of thing which makes for happy dreams.

This ledge pocket was shaped like an hourglass. The fish had come from the upper half, so I aimed my next cast downstream to the lower half. I worked the lure in the same manner as on the first cast. There was no watery explosion to interrupt the katydid chorus. In fact, I heard nothing. It seemed that a fish suddenly had the lure and was hanging on, so I struck. Again pulsating life was felt through the arched rod and taut line. In due time another big bass came to net. These two fish were almost exactly the same size, but how different were their strikes under identical conditions. Were these strikes brought about by hunger, curiosity, pugnacity, irritability, or some combination thereof? An answer cannot be given with certainty. Bass psychology is an inexact science.

The favorite surface lure of Ron Kommer, a talented and experienced muskie fisherman, is the smallest size Mud Puppy of the C. C. Roberts Bait Company of Mosinee, Wisconsin. With the slightest pressure, the tail of this ¾-ounce lure spins as the head moves right and left.

New in 1972 was the Fincheroo by Robfin Industries of Scottsdale, Arizona. This unique floater has a hollow head or big collar and a prop at the tail end. When jerked, the lure bores into the surface, causing a waterspout as the propeller churns at the other end.

The magic hour on a river or lake is the time between sundown and dark. This is the great period for the surface lure for bass and muskies. Only the less-convenient time of dawn is as consistently good.

BABY POPPER
by Shakespeare Co.
This lure was ahead of its time, since
spinning was not yet known in America
and it was lighter than those employed by
most bait casters. This surface lure floats
in a vertical position at rest because the
tail is thin. With rod-tip manipulation, the
lure levels and the large face makes a
plip-plip sound, at times creating a large
bubble which explodes.

BABY POPPER
homemade, by Charles Fox,
with inverted rubber skirt. When one is
fortunate enough by chance or design to
intercept the seventeen-year-locust infestation in bass country, he would do well to
fish a *Baby Popper* decorated with a rubber
skirt. The skirt is cemented around the
body of the lure in a position so that in
casting it folds back, offering little air resistance. Once on the water, the ends loop
out from the body.

BABY POPPERS
two homemade lures
beside the old original by the Shakespeare
Co.

BARNEY GOOGLE
by Jim Donely.
Jim Donely produced a second surface
bait; this one he called *Barney Google*
after a funny-paper character of the 20s.
The plug was a tendency to swing attrac-
tively around on the surface, as the long
prop splatters the water.

BLOOPER
by Paul C. Lott of Owensboro, Kentucky
is an interesting innovation of 1971. This
fine popping-face, rubber-leg surface bait
is made specifically to get into the places
where the bass can escape the direct bright
rays of the sun, such as timber, weedbeds,
and lily pads.

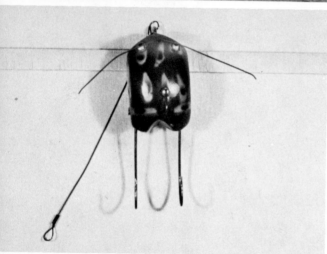

BUG
by the Creek Chub Bait Co.
This Creek Chub *Bug* of the early 30s
combined a wire trace, weed guards, a
pork-rind loop, and an ingenious hooking
arrangement. Its creator obviously had
hazzard fishing in mind when he came up
with this one.

CHARGER
by the Ketchmore Bait Co.
Jim Omdoll, the genial proprietor of the
Ketchmore Bait Co. of Palmyra, Wisconsin, designed and produced this lure. It is
attractive, well hooked yet hook protected,
and with pulling power for target fishing,
it's a great one for fishing the pad fields.

CRAZY CRAWLER
by James Heddon's Sons
in its two sizes.

CREEPER
by the Phillips Tackle Co.
was made in an Erie, Pennsylvania, work-shop for local muskie fishing; then there followed a bass-size model. It is now produced for its owner, Jim Vallentine, Pennsylvania muskie-fishing fish warden, by the Phillips Tackle Co.

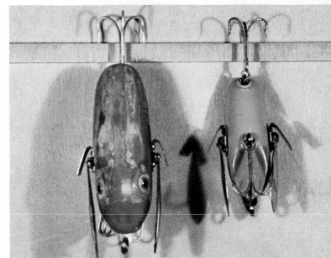

CRY BABY
by Ridge Runner.
This lure bobs and weaves on the surface as a back prop splatters and the skirt on the treble hook acts alive.

DASHER
by Fred Arbogast Co.
The Arbogast *Dasher* with front prop removed and a second prop added to tail.

DOWAGIAC
by James Heddon Co.
Late in the 19th century it was discovered that bass could be attracted just as well as they could be deceived. Jim Heddon designed and placed on the market his *Dowagiac*, which was his first plug.

DUCKLING
by an unknown maker.
The *Duckling* is cute. Should more be said?

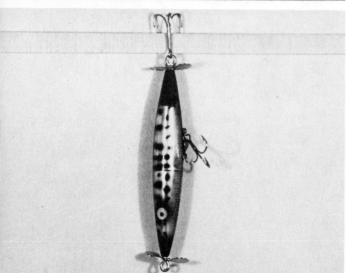

DYING QUIVER
by James Heddon's Sons.
This *Dying Quiver* is equipped with small, light props.

DYING QUIVER
by James Heddon's Sons.
Another innovation of Homer Circle's for Heddon involved a new and different principle in lures. *The Dying Quiver* is very sensitive to rodstip action. It bobs and flashes and even jumps.

JOE FARCHT LURES.
Joe Farcht of Mount Wolf, Pennsylvania, produced an imposing array of both surface and sinking lures, all excellent. But Joe and his wife were creator, manufacturer, sales force and at the same time avid anglers, with the result that the lures did not receive the distribution and promotion they deserved. To further complicate matters, cheaper-to-manufacture plastic plugs were forging ahead.

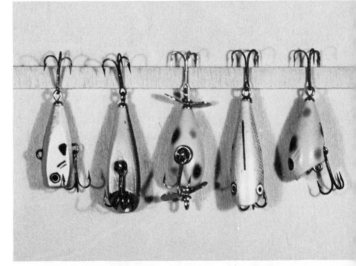

FINCHEROO
by Robfin of Scottsdales, Arizona.
New in '72 was *Fincheroo,* and it is different too. The great hole in the head spits and spews water every time the nose submerges under pressure, and the prop purrs as the lure rocks. And if this is not enough, a played-out fish can be lifted out of the water by the angler hooking a forefinger in the ring head of the lure.

FISHCAKE
by Charles Helin.
Charlie Helin added to his *Flatfish* line a small surface lure with a tricky propeller and hook spreader, which he called *Fish Cake*. This lure has pulling power for good casting.

FLIP TOP
by Burke.
Burke lures are unique in that they are made of beautifully painted soft rubber. Construction is such that hooks and screw-eyes are firm. *Flip Top*—a combination popper face and prop tail—is a fine surface lure, this one bearing muskie tooth marks.

FLUTTER-FIN
by The Worth Co.
The *Flutter-Fin*, a surface bait, encompasses a combination of unique features, which make it a different sort of lure.

GAR
by an unknown Canadian maker

is made in two sizes, the larger being a floater at rest and a great casting lure for muskies when a top-water lure is in order.

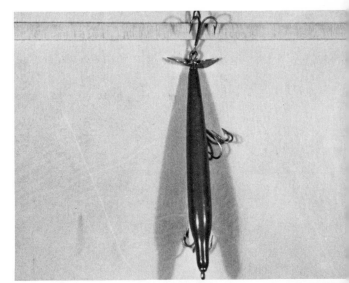

WALTER HARDEN SPECIAL
by James Heddon's Sons.

Walter Harden became deeply involved with Florida bass fishing, where he experienced great success. Some of the bass he was catching in Lake Apopka on his remodeled lures did not look like the usual southern largemouth, and for several years were adjudged to be smallmouth bass. While using a lure like the one shown, he broke the world record and Heddon put the lure on the market. Later the authorities agreed that his fish were a strain or color phase of largemouth bass, and the record could not stand. The biggest of his bass was mounted, only to be stolen from his gas station in Pennsylvania.

HAZARD FISHING SPECIAL
homemade by Charles Fox.

If ever there was a weedless lure, this is it.

HULA POPPER
by Fred Arbogast Co.
incorporates a plunking face and an undulating skirt especially made for this purpose of cut rubber on a piece of rubber tubing.

HUSTLER
by Ridge Runner

is a neat little surface lure of great merit. It comes in a variety of finishes, and the paint jobs are good.

INJURED MINNOWS
by different companies.
Many of the manufacturers of lures in the closing years of the wooden-bass-plug era tried their hands at floaters with one or two propellers. In various lengths, thicknesses, and weights this type has been called *Crippled Minnow, Injured Minnow, SOS, Torpedo, Surf Oreno,* etc.

JERSEY WOW
by Jim Donley.

A native of New Jersey, Jim Donley designed the *Jersey Wow*, a surface bait with swimming arms that made it totally different from any previously seen. After marketing it for a decade, he sold the rights to Heddon, who has produced it to his day in two sizes under the name of *Crazy Crawler.*

JITTERBUG
by Fred Arbogast Co.

While sitting in a canoe, Fred Arbogast dreamed up his *Jitterbug*, a type of lure totally different from his realistic, singlehook, wobbling spoon, *Tin Liz*, which was designed as a deceiver for distance casting. *Tin Liz* was short-lived but *Jitterbug*, a surface attractor, outlived Fred and today prospers under the loving care of Dick Kotis. A great surface bait, particularly for night bass fishing.

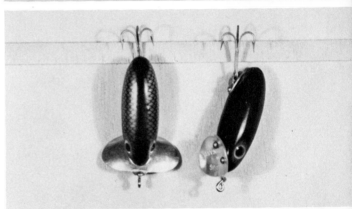

JITTERBUG
by Fred Arbogast Co.

During the seasons encompassed by World War II, when metal was hard to come by, *Jitterbug* was equipped with a colored plastic face. This proved to be a temporary measure, for the lighter-weight plastic would not make the lure shoulder into the surface to emit the famous Jitterbug gurgle.

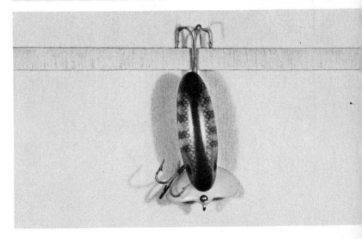

JITTERBUG
with Hula Popper skirt
by Fred Arbogast Co.

A screweye is inserted on the top of the tail of a *Jitterbug*, then a *Hula Popper* skirt is placed over it to produce the maximum in liveliness.

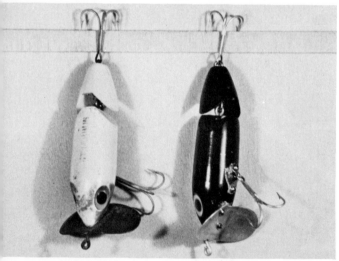

JOINTED JITTERBUG
by Fred Arbogast Co.

Dick Kotis, the genial boss of the Arbogast Company, has produced a jointed model of the famous *Jitterbug*.

K9 AND BASS SNATCHER
by Ridge Runner.

Ben Bacon, an ardent bass fisherman and movie-maker, heads up Ridge Runner lures in Shreveport, Louisiana. The *K9* is an attractive example of the trim crippled-minnow type. His *Bass Snatcher*, of the same type, is tremendous in size. What he may not know is that they are worthy muskie plugs.

LUM SURFACE LURE
by The James Heddon Co.

One of the early Heddon innovations was called the *Lum 210 Surface*. Its creator latched onto night fishing and the luminous finish early in the lure-casting game.

MOSS HOPPER
by Four Rivers Tackle Co.

John Aldridge of Four Rivers Tackle Co., Greenwood, Mississippi, has developed this unique surface lure. Although it sinks, the *Moss Hopper* is designed to crawl across and through protruding weedbeds. The trick is not to strike until the bass has broken through the vegetation and mouthed the lure.

MUD PUPPY or RIVER PUP
by C. C. Roberts.

Many lure casters for muskies know about the *Mud Puppy* by C. C. Robert of Mosinee, Wisconsin. This ¾-oz. surface bait is called *River Pup* by its creator. It is a very special muskie lure for the caster.

PAD JUMPER
by Bob Bates.
This lure is balanced in such a way that when it lands on its back it automatically rolls over.

PADDLER
by the Shakespeare Co.
combined imitation legs and feet in the form of spinners on swivels with a double hook, hook points up. The result was pad-crawling ability.

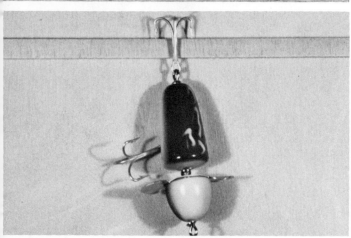

PFLUEGER GLOBE LURE
now made by Shakespeare.
This tried and tested lure was the continuation of the *Decker Bait*, one of the first lures invented. It was advertised in the 1915 William Mills & Son Catalog.

PHILLIPS LURES
Test Lures by the Phillips Tackle Co.
After this author gave George Phillips some of his homemade lures as models, George experimented with bodies by gluing two hollow parts together, then painting them and attaching appropriate hardware. The ones pictured here were trial lures.

PLUMMER'S FLOATING FROG
by Harrison Co.

This frog was especially designed to be fished in the pad fields.

PLUNKERS
by The Creek Chub Bait Co.

Plunker was the first of the popping-type surface lures. The ones pictured are the more recent baby sizes.

POCONO CEDER PLUG
by J. Lester Boorse.

This *Pocono Cedar Plug* was given to the author by its maker, J. Lester Boorse. It was made after this accomplished gunsmith lost his eyesight. He now makes very special and beautiful coffee tables.

RATTLER
homemade by Charlie Fox.

The head is hollow with several loose BB shot that rattle about in a hollow section sealed off with plastic wood. This homemade *Rattler* (1958) stays in a vertical position at rest; with rod-tip manipulation it is made to level and rock.

SPIRAL LURES
*by the T & T Co. of
Sanitiria Springs, N. Y.*
The two models of *Spiral Fishing Lures* are unique among lures. These sensitive surface lures, designed by Mahlon Treaster, fish wonderfully well.

SURFACE BAIT
by Grudebrod.
The Grudebrod concept of a fine surface bait incorporates a sloping face, a tail prop, and a flashing finish under clear plastic.

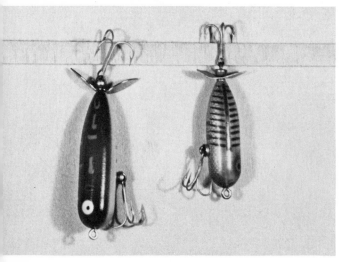

TINY TORPEDO
by James Heddon's Sons
fast became a favorite of the river fishermen for smallmouth bass. It is made in three sizes, the largest of which is 3/8 oz. Its introduction was the year 1940 or thereabouts.

TOP 'N' POP
by The Creek Chub Bait Co.
This lure combines weaving action with
tail wiggle.

WALKIE TALKIE
by an unknown manufacturer
was a tricky ¼-oz. surface bait that deserves to be rejuvenated. The sloping concave face made it a talker, and the trim flat
tail made it a walker.

WISE LURES
homemade surface lures
by Jack Wise of the Poconos.
These were unusual in the early days of
spinning when the available lures were,
for the most part, foreign-made metal
ones.

The Floating Wobbler

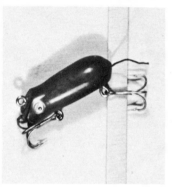

See picture section
beginning on page 37.

The pioneer plug casters were boat fishermen working the shorelines and pad fields of midwestern lakes. Kentucky, Wisconsin, and Minnesota were hotbeds. The standard early lure was an underwater swimmer that floated at rest.

Three of the great lures from the 20s that have survived into the era of mass production are the Creek Chub Pikie Minnow, the Heddon Vamp, and the South Bend Bass Oreno. All three have been good to me. The first muskie I caught casting was taken on a Pikie Minnow, and my first pike took a Vamp. A Bass Oreno was responsible for a most interesting series of incidents.

Back in the 1930s a friend and I were fishing in the Kawartha Lake region out of the town of Babcaygeon, Ontario. It was the usual thing for the guides to bring in their charges at about 6:00 p.m. for dinner at the Rockland House. Thus the magic hour was wasted, and considering this a great loss, I took my bait-casting outfit for an evening walk. The path that I followed happened to lead to the town docks, where a heavy shoot of water belched from Sturgeon Lake through a gateway into Pigeon Lake. The wide, flat top of the dam was a good place to cast from. The shoot spent its course in about 100 feet and fanned out into an attractive, mysterious-looking pool. What to me was then a good long cast would just about cover the fan of water.

In a box in my pocket were three plugs—the big three so far as I was concerned—a Pikie, a Vamp, and a Bass Oreno. I chose the last of the three because it is the most castable. This one happened to have a blue-scale finish, no doubt the first blue plug sold commercially. I had never used it before.

After a couple of warm-up casts, I tossed the lure to the farthest extremity of the fan. Instead of reeling in, I clamped down on the line and permitted the action of the current to bring the lure across the tail of the fan. This was a well-balanced Bass Oreno, and it flashed from side to side as it swam across the fishy-looking area. Then there was a different, much bigger flash, and an instant later I felt the strike. In the heavy water the muskie felt strong and put on a fine show, jumping twice. By moving off the abutment I was able to get to the water's edge, where in due time I beached the fish.

My mistake was in taking this muskie back to the hotel, where the fishermen and guides had gathered for the usual evening confab. Naturally I had to tell where and how the fish was taken.

The next evening, as soon as dinner was over, I grabbed my rod and headed for what I thought of now as "the fan pool." About half the fishermen and guides walked over to see what I was up to. I caught another muskie and a bass, both on the blue-scale Bass Oreno, which I later retired and still have.

On the third evening it seemed as though everybody at the hotel came over, and my guide had to make casting room for me by keeping the people at a safe distance. Evening three produced muskie number three.

Things went very much the same way for the rest of the trip. Certainly evening fishing at the fan was the cream of my fishing vacation that year. Often I wonder what the place looks like today, for I never got back. Someone told me that there is now a fish refuge at the mouth of Pigeon Creek, where as a boy with my Dad I caught my first 'lunge.

Joe Pflueger, of the Pflueger Fishing Tackle Company, also fished out of Babcaygeon. He had recently added a new lure to his line, a version of the floating underwater wabbler which he called Pal O'Mine. It featured a new and different type of metal lip. About the same time, a novel idea in lure design combined with a new idea in lure color appeared on the market. Carter's Black Joe looked like the head of a bird with its mouth open. It was streamlined to cast, and its side-to-side underwater wabble was just about right.

As a fifteen year old, I attended a boy's camp on Sebago Lake in Maine where there were only four activities—fishing, baseball, swimming, and eating. That summer I bought an amazing-looking plug at the general store in South Casco. Heddon's

Game Fisher was jointed in two places, and its underwater wiggle was deep and lifelike. Although it was oversize for bass, every now and then one would hit it and get hooked. I still have this green-scale antique. Over the years the white belly has turned a beautiful ivory color. Along with it is the baby version, which has but one joint.

I was also sorry to see another floater of the 20s pass along. The Rush Tango Swimming Minnow, made in two sizes, was unique in its day because the lure was streamlined to cast like a bullet, its sloping face made it the deepest runner of all, and its action was lively and erratic. It had no metal lip, and today, as in the past, the blank can be worked out on a lathe and the face cut with a saw, then buffed. In recent years three similar lures, Lazy Ike, Hot Shot, and Tad Polly, have appeared.

I came to fish the great old Rush Tango for northern pike, and now and then a fine bass would hit it. One of the three biggest smallmouths I have ever hooked took the large size in a red head and yellow body. A great round boulder was barely submerged at August water level. My cast was to the rock, and as the sloping nose started to take the lure down and start it wiggling, there came a terrific strike and a sickening snap. Twice the great fish jumped with the detached plug. The bass had literally taken the lure, but the next day I got it back as it floated along the shore some 150 feet from the rock. This was in the days when a lure was tied directly to the braided line, and tip-guide friction at the start of the cast soon weakened the first six inches of line. The idea was to cut this section off every hour or two and retie. I paid the price of postponing this operation too long.

As time passed there followed Heddon's Basser and Luck 13, and Charlie Helin's very active but hard to cast Flatfish with its new hook-spreader arrangement. These three lures are still on the market. Since the promotion and popularization of spinning, both Rebel and Rapala have introduced their long, trim, sensitive, violent wabblers, with the bright new-type finishes.

In the past, particularly during the great wooden-lure era, the floating underwater wabbler was the most common lure type. Today the majority of lures are sinkers.

ABU HI-LOW
by Garcia.

The five stages at which the *Abu Hi-Lo* operates are controlled by the easily adjustable mouthpiece. It was made in two sizes, the larger of which floats, while the smaller is a sinker. Some consider the larger one the perfect underwater wobbler for pike and muskies. Sales terminated due to a disagreement between the Swedish manufacturer and the American distributor—a great pity.

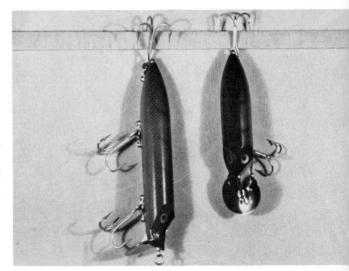

BASS ORENO
by the South Bend Bait Co.

When a floating, underwater, wobbling lure designed and made by Ivar Hennings came on the market, it was the start of the South Bend Bait Co., now a part of Gladding. Pictured here is the initial model *Bait Oreno* along with *a Babe Oreno* and a *Midge Oreno*. The introduction of the three sizes spanned a period of twenty-five years, and all are still in production. The *Bass Oreno* was the first lure to pass the million mark in sales.

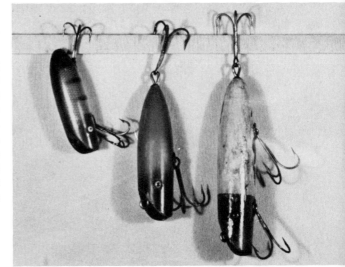

BASS ORENO
by The South Bend Bait Co.

Hennings was also probably the innovator of the scale finish. This particular lure, which dates from the late 20s, has a blue scale, yet in this day we associate blue lures for game fish as something relatively new.

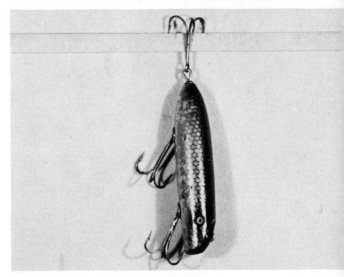

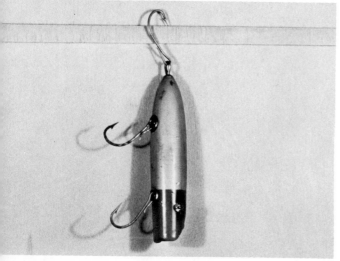

BASS ORENO
by The South Bend Bait Co.

For a time the state of New Jersey had a three-hook-point law. The answer to it by the South Bend Bait Co. was a specially equipped *Bass Oreno.*

BATES MIDGET
homemade by Bob Bates.

This *Midget* is a fine design by Bob Bates and an excellent floating underwater wobbler.

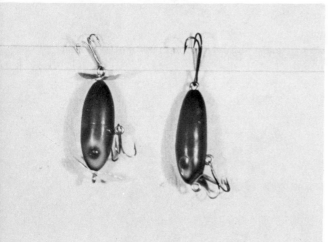

BUG-A-BOO BABYS
by Wright and McGill.

The two lures pictured here may represent a milestone in the craft of luremaking in America. Wright and McGill made these two plastics expressly for spin fishing, no doubt with bass in mind. The little, green-eyed, black wobbler on the right was named the *Bug-A-Boo Baby.*

CRAB WIGGLER
by The James Heddon Co.
was an inverted version of the first Heddon lure in that the metal collar was reversed to become a mouthpiece. The action was narrow and violent, and the lure had good pulling power. It was advertised in the 1915 William Mills & Son Catalog.

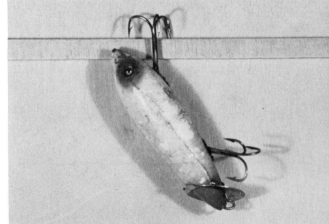

FATS-O BY STROM
*"O" models are produced
by various manufacturers.*
In different models the "O" refers to the pregnant minnow shape. The original, a homemade model, made its reputation in the Midsouth by winning some bass tournaments. The commercial lures have built-in rattles, similar to the *Rattle Bug* of the 40s.

FINNISH WARRIOR
by an unknown maker.
The ¼-oz. *Finnish Warrior* is a surface lue with an action the maker refers to as "fin-fan."

FLATFISH
by Charlie Helin.
This lure has violent action, offers considerable resistance on the retrieve, and features hook spreaders and small light-wire hooks. Because it lacks pulling power, it is basically a trolling lure.
Fig. 107

FLATFISH
homemade lure by an unknown maker.
It employs the *Flatfish* principle but is beefed up to cast.

FLIP FROG
by Webber Lifelike Fly Co.
is an underwater wobbler.

LUNG FROG
by James Heddon's Sons.

The "plaster" frog represented an attempt by Heddon to go realistic. Possibly this was the first casting lure made of a material other than wood or metal. It was advertised in the 1927 William Mills & Son catalog.

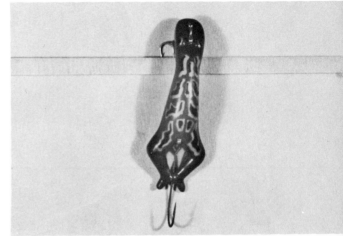

GAME FISHER
by James Heddon Co.

Another first for the great innovator, Jim Heddon, was this jointed plug. The first model had two joints and three parts; the baby size had one joint and two parts. The larger of the two was probably first sold in 1922.

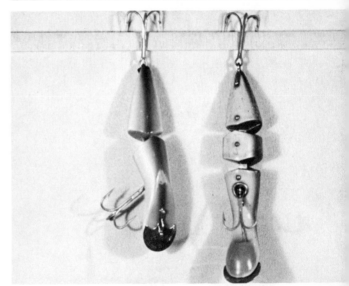

HOT SHOT
by Eddie Pope.

Eddie Pope of Valencia, California, placed on the market his *Hot Shot*, a floating underwater wobbler that made its mark among the ardent lure casters. He followed this up with a sister plug, *Fishback*, which promptly became a popular lure for Great Lakes Cohos, an introduced species.

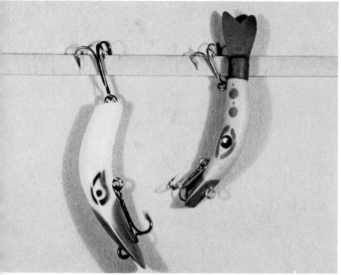

LAZY IKE
by the Lazy Ike Corporation.

Long lower-jawed *Lazy Ike*, made in Fort Dodge, Iowa, has plenty of wiggle and pulling power for good casting and effective fishing.

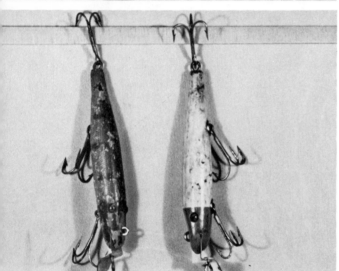

PICKIE MINNOWS
by The Creek Chub Bait Co.

The year of the birth of the *Pikie Minnow* was possibly 1924, and it marked the rise of the Creek Chub Bait Co. of Garrett, Indiana. The first *Pikies* had two possible places for line attachment: the one on the metal lip, which gave the lure a fast wobbling action in a narrow path at a depth of about two feet; the one at the head screweye made it ride deeper with a leisurely wobble.

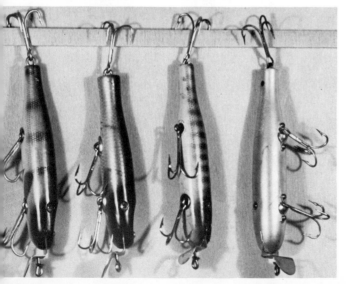

PICKIE MINNOWS
by The Creek Chub Co.

A family of *Pikie Minnows*. Now and then the Creek Chub people slightly altered the shape of the body. This lure holds the honor of having taken the world-record muskie.

JOINTED PIKIE MINNOW
by The Creek Chub Bait Co.

After the *Pikie Minnow* was solidly established as a popular fish getter, the Creek Chub people introduced it in a jointed version. In effectiveness and popularity it promptly took its place beside its illustrious forerunner.

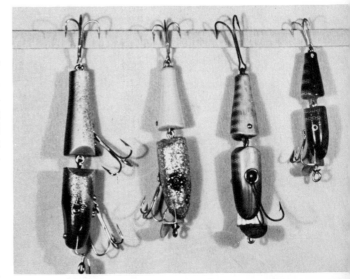

RAPALA
by the Normark Corporation.

One of the last of the wooden lures came from Finland and were made for both bait-casting and spinning. Trim, extremely sensitive, and beautiful describes *Rapala* lures. Made of balsa wood, these lures have a shaft running through the body to anchor the sharp hooks. *Rapala* reached a new dimension in flashing finishes.

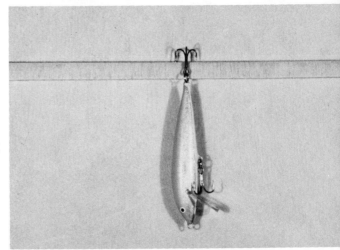

REBEL
by The Plastics Research and Development Corp.

The beautiful, trim, sensitive *Rebel*, the sharp hooks of which are loose on split rings, features brilliant flashing finishes and a snappy wiggle. This popular lure is a product of Fort Smith, Arkansas, a tremendous all-round lure from a tremendous bigmouth bass state.

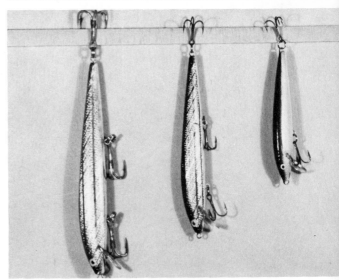

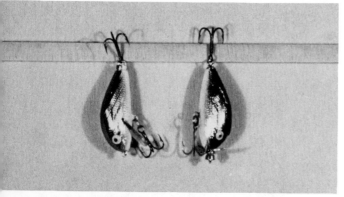

REBEL HUMPBACKS
*by Plastics Research and
Development Corp.*
deviated from the original long trim lure
in order to add variety. No doubt this was
done with bass and pan fish in mind. Pictured is a hump-back underwater wobbler
and surface bait.

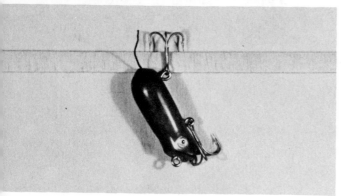

SWIMMING MOUSE
by the Shakespeare Co.
has been an effective lure for four decades.
It is one of the few early plugs that lends
itself to the skim-and-swim approach.

RUSH TANGO MINNOW
*is the original swimming, diving wobbler
bait (1917)" . . . sketch and quote from a
May 1917 advertisement run by J. K. Rush
of Syracuse, N. Y., in the old National
Sportsman magazine, Boston, Mass.*

This creation by Rush was the first all-
wood deep swimmer. Furthermore, it pos-
sessed great pulling power for good
casting. The lure faded away in the 30s,
following the passing of its maker.

SWIMMING MINNOW
by Rush Tango.

Pictured are two sizes of the great old Rush Tango. It was advertised in the 1915 William Mills & Son Catalog.

TEASE ORENO
by The South Bend Bait Co.

The most violent contorting wobble of all is probably that of the old South Bend *Tease Oreno.* The cup face and the bowed body work together, each supplementing the other. Here is an idea for the home lure-maker.

VAMP
by James Heddon's Sons

whether by accident or design, became the competitor of the *Pikie Minnow,* and that situation still prevails. Although the two have different mouthpieces and line attachment arrangements, the swimming actions are similar—side-to-side in a narrow path at a two-foot depth.

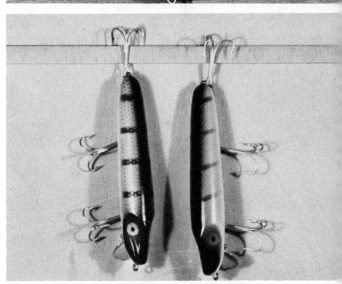

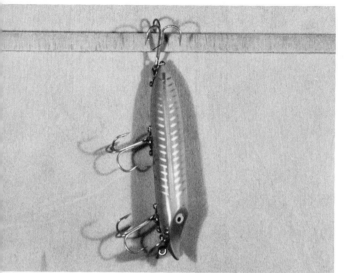

VAMP
by James Heddon's Sons.
When Heddon was converting from wood to plastic, the *Vamp* followed *River Runt* in a plastic version. The translucent effect was called Share Finish.

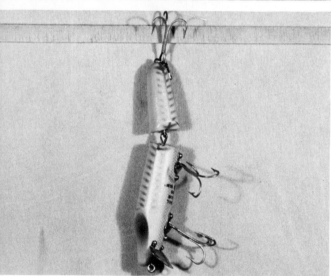

JOINTED VAMP
by James Heddon's Sons.

Heddon produced the popular *Vamp* in a jointed model employing a hinging device different from that used by their old *Game Fisher* and Creek Chub's new jointed *Pikie*.

WATER DOG and HELLBENDER
by the Bomber Bait Co. of Gainesville, Texas.

The Bomber Bait Company produced this pair of deep wobblers similar in nature. Both *Water Dog* and *Hellbender* dig down with fast reeling. These are important bass lures for drop-off fishing, particularly at frost time.

There are two specific situations that call for the sinking lure with side-to-side swimming action—walleye fishing and bass fishing in the fall where the bass stack up for the winter.

This lure concept was a child of the late 1930s and came at the start of the era of plastics. Heddon, the great pioneering company, then placed on the market something new and different—a translucent, plastic sinker they called the River Runt Spook. They followed it with a River Runt with a tremendous metal lip—the "Go Deeper" model.

South Bend then quickly produced an opaque plastic sinker with a metal lip, which they named Fish-O-Bite.

For a relatively short time during the 1940s a sinking model of the Water Scout was available.

Homer Circle, a rabid lure fisherman, was then a vice president of Heddon as well as lure designer. Later he wrote a book, *How To Plug Fish*. He is currently the fishing editor of *Sports Afield*. From the day he walked into the Heddon office at Dowagiac, Michigan, with a homemade walnut plug of a new design he has been a lure designer and tester. It was he who came up with the first "sonic" lures. He discovered that placing the line-attachment screw eye on the top of the neck of a narrow fish-shaped plug will cause the lure to vibrate rapidly on the retrieve. This vibration creates noise, hence the name "sonic." After the first of these lures was developed, Homer sent me a beautiful sample with my name in the finish. There followed other versions of both sinking and floating sonic lures, the Bayou Boogie by Whopper Stopper being well known.

The largest smallmouth bass I ever saw was caught under odd circumstances by a friend using a sinking wabbler. It was

Sinking Wobblers

See picture section beginning on page 49.

bluebird weather in late November. If any ducks were flying on the Susquehanna on such a day they would be very high, so Nip Boyer took his plugging outfit as well as his shotgun. The water below was big, deep, and beautiful, a well-known walleye spot. In due course Nip gave up on the ducks and turned to the casting outfit. He cast his River Runt Spook downstream, let it sink to the bottom in ten feet of water, then made a slow and steady retrieve, feeling the lazy wabble of the plug through the rod. Something hit the lure, and Nip struck back. He was sure he was into a huge walleye, for there was no jumping or running, just a great deal of very heavy resistance. When the fish finally came to the boat, Nip almost fell overboard, for there before him was the greatest river smallmouth he had ever seen, a heavily built lunker of seven and a quarter pounds.

One of the most violent fishing arguments I ever witnessed was between a new plug fisherman and an old troller, the troller being basically a walleye fisherman. It was the troller's contention that his beloved "Susquehanna salmon" (walleyed pike) could be caught only by trolling a Junebug spinner ahead of a salamander or a bunch of nightcrawlers. The caster maintained that these fish could be taken on plugs, not that he had ever so caught one, but he had heard and read about it.

Incidentally, at that time, which was before the day of the large new impoundments, the world-record walleye according to the Pflueger catalogue was sixteen pounds. Hanging in the American House in Highspire along the Susquehanna was a big one that was supposed to have weighed eighteen pounds. It had been caught at Hawk Rock, today a famous muskie sector of the mile-wide river.

It was to Hawk Rock that the troller took the caster. The boat was anchored upstream from a deep pocket in the great limestone ledges. The newly introduced River Runt Spook was cast downstream and permitted to settle before the start of the retrieve.

The caster made his point, for it did not take him long to catch two respectable walleyes. It is interesting to note that the incident revolutionized trolling in the area, though trollers added their own refinement. They came to employ a floating woo-den River Runt ahead of a ¾-ounce pear-shaped sinker on a weak dropper. The idea was to row slowly so the lead bumped along the bottom with the buoyant lure riding not far off bottom. When the lead caught on bottom, the weak dropper line would be broken, and thus the sinker and not the lure was lost.

Recently Jim Omdoll of the Ketchmore Bait Company has introduced an especially fine deep-running lure, the Shore River Shiner, which is available in thirteen finishes in ¼- and ½-ounce sizes.

If we are going to put up with and adhere to rules, here are two good ones—fish deep with a sinking wabbler for walleyes at all times, and do the same in the fall at the stack-up places of bass.

BEETLE
by the Creek Chub Bait Co.
The old-time short-lived Creek Chub *Beetle,* with its *Pikie Minnow* lip and trailer hook with pearl spinner, is unique and remains thought-provoking for the do-it-yourself clan.

CISCO KID
by Cisco Kid of Boco Raton, Florida.
In the ½-oz. size it is excellent for wal-leyes and in the ¾-oz.model it is a good lure for pike and muskies, even though it was made primarily for big southern bass and salt-water fish.

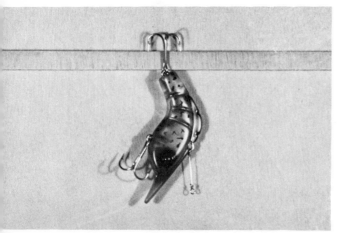

CRAW SHRIMP
by James Heddon's Sons.
Heddon applied the sonic principle to realism, and the resulting *Craw Shrimp* is true to nature and excellent for salt-water fishing.

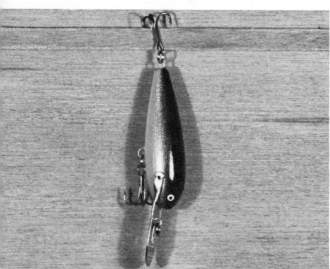

DEEP DIVER 90
by Rapala
is basically for drop-off fishing for bass and for walleyes.

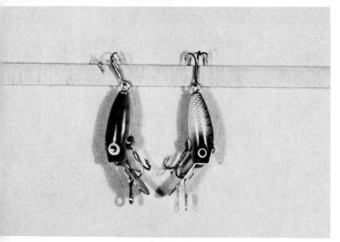

DEEP-R-DOODLE
by the Wood Manufacturing Co.
The Wood Manufacturing Co. of Eldorado, Arkansas, tested the market with this tiny, deep swimming underwater wobbler. This was a good lure for walleyes and for cold water bass.

FISH-O-BITE
by South Bend Bait Co.

The South Bend Bait Co. produced the second plastic lure, this one being opaque and smaller than the *River Runt*. Although it was a fine sinking wobbler, *Fish-O-Bite* was on the market only a few seasons.

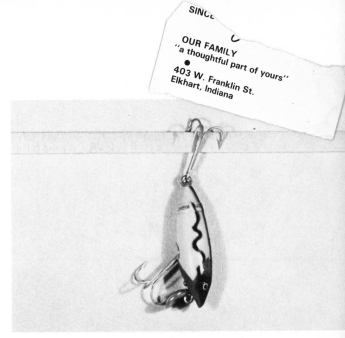

GO DEEPER RIVER RUNT
by James Heddon's Sons.

Heddon attached a massive lower lip to *River Runt* and called it the *Go-Deeper*. It made its mark as a prime walleye lure.

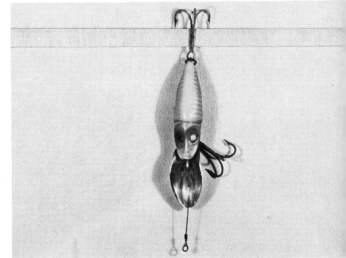

GRUMPY and DOPEY
by the Shakespeare Co.

In the late 30s Shakespeare produced two tiny but heavy lures named after Snow White's dwarfs. Both were sinking underwater wobblers. Note the use of metal on the underside of *Dopey*.

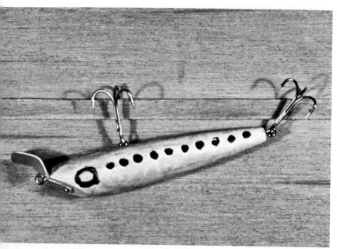

JINX
by Charles Fox.
This lure is a fine muskie and pike plug.

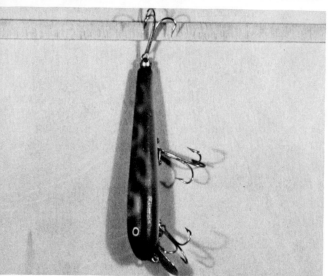

LATINOWOBBLER
Eddie Latiano of Elwood City, Pennsylvania,
makes this wobbler, each variation being numbered. He also sells his wooden version of the defunct *Super Spook*. These are two excellent muskie lures.

LOOSE-EYE SHAD
by Cotton Cordell.
A sonic lure, might qualify as a deciever in the reservoirs of the Midsouth where the gizzard shad prevails. This is a fine lure for the bigger white bass as well as for largemouths. It is manufactured in Hot Springs, Arkansas, in the heart of the reservoir bass country.

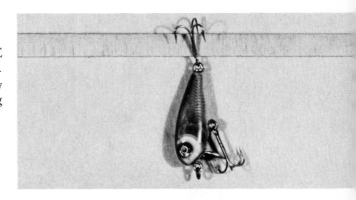

MIDGE
by Barracuda of Florida.
Barracuda tested the market with this tiny solid-plastic lure, salt-water species being the main target.

MR. WHISKERS
by Garcia.
New in '73, is a deep wobbling lure.

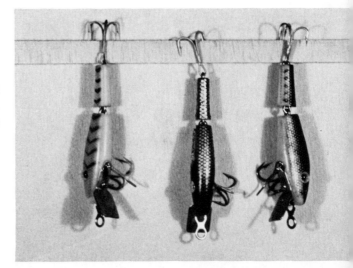

PAN FISH MASTER
by L & S Bait Co.
is a worthy bass and walleye lure, in spite of its name.

RIVER RUNT SPOOK
by James Heddon's Sons.
It may have been coincidental that the era of the wooden plug and World War II practically terminated together, and that the era of the plastic lure and spinning in America grew up together. The great lure-pioneering firm founded by Jim Heddon produced the *River Runt* in plastic. This innovation of 1933 is a semitranslucent sinking underwater wobbler with an air chamber. At the time of its introduction it was considered a small lure. Spinning—which features the use of small lures—was then unknown in America.

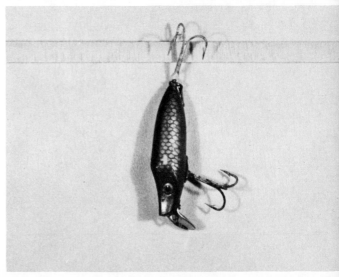

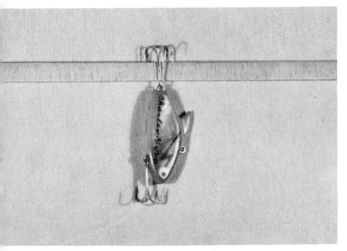

SONIC LURE
by James Heddon's Sons.
While Homer Circle was the lure designer for Heddon, he initiated the sonic-style lure. The screweye on the back of the neck in conjunction with the flat minnow-shape body produce a violent narrow-path action, almost a vibration. Its creator had the name of this writer inscribed on one before the finishing coat was applied and presented it as a Christmas present in the year 1956.

WATER SCOUT
by the Wood Manufacturing Co.
came in beautiful finishes in both floating and sinking models. Note the use of metal.

The identity of this solid-plastic lure has been lost, but it incorporates several novel features. The shape of the mold with the sheet-thin tail and fins, the method of jointing, the enlarged scoop, the hook attachment in plastic, the bug eyes, and the finish are all innovative.

In the shadows of the past a glittering tidbit adorned the showcases and shelves of the hardware and sporting goods stores up and down the Susquehanna watershed. It was the local plug for stream smallmouths. There were other lures for sale, such as Pikie Minnows, Bass Orenos, Vamps, and Skinner and Pflueger spoons, but those were for the fellows who went to Canada for muskies and pike. The lure that enjoyed the local monopoly was Jim Heddon's Dowagiac. Heddon must have liked it very much, for he named it after his hometown in Michigan.

Although the smaller Dowagiac weighed ½ ounce, it was only two inches long. In the front was a very sensitive and well-made propeller. There was an abnormally small treble hook on each side and another on the tail. The longer ⅝-ounce model had a prop fore and aft. These two lures had entirely different underwater swimming actions. The smaller wabbled some, whereas the larger followed a straight course. Both were aerodynamically sound, hence good casters. The speed of the retrieve controlled the running depth. With either one it was an easy matter to make the lure climb to the surface to avoid shallow ledges by speeding up the retrieve and lifting the rod tip.

Don Martin, a fishing partner of old became well-known around the state for having broken the Pennsylvania record for brown trout with a fifteen and a half pounder. (His record has since been broken several times.) He lived along the Susquehanna and did a great deal of stream fishing for bass. On one occasion we made a trip in August to Pine Creek, a large upstate feeder of the Susquehanna. The Big Pine is long and wide, and it drops rapidly through rocky mountainous country, making for great pools and long flats with riffles, slicks, and glides in between.

Sinking Propeller Lures

See picture section beginning on page 58

Don and I carefully worked several beautiful pools, but we caught nothing and saw nothing. We drifted apart for several hours. When we met for lunch I was greeted with the question, "Well, have you figured it out?"

When I informed Don that I hadn't, he looked like the cat that had swallowed the canary. Half curious, half sarcastic, I asked, "How many dozen did you catch?"

"Three," he said.

"Three or three dozen?" I persisted.

"I said 'three' and you said 'dozen' and the answer is both."

"That I must see."

"All right," he said, "after lunch you will see—right in the stretch you've been fishing."

This made me so curious that I tried to rush the issue, but Don wasn't to be pushed.

Finally we left our flat rock in the shade and started up the creek. The cool water felt good as it penetrated my sodden stockings and trousers. Before us was a beautiful deep pool. Much to my surprise Don bypassed it. Then, like a bird dog inhaling a light scent, he pussyfooted to a point on the side of a riffle and stopped. "Here's where they are, in the aerated riffles, not the pools."

His cast was not made to the riffle proper; it was aimed at the shallow water to one side of the channel. The little frog-finish Dowagiac hit with a flat smack, and Don's rapid retrieve held it near the surface above the menacing rocks. Three waves converged on the lure, and a small bass was promptly hooked, played, and released.

This demonstration was a revelation to me, but the most remarkable feature of the day was what followed. Twice that afternoon in my presence Don hooked two bass at one time, on one occasion catching the pair and the other time losing one. The Dowagiac was perfect for this situation.

In the early 40s the Shakespeare Company produced a chunky little propeller lure with two props and two treble hooks which they called the Midget Spinner. This lure took the Susquehanna casters by storm, including those who fished the

Maryland section of the river below the massive Conowingo Dam.

In my judgment, the sinking propeller lure is the most effective type of lure to use when raindrops are hitting the water. As long as I live I'll never forget an afternoon spent on some great Susquehanna ledge water. The river was low and clear, and the water was warm. Wading wet felt good on that hot, sticky August dog day.

For two hours I tried one lure after another and never had a strike. By late afternoon, storm clouds gathered in the west and thunderheads sounded their warning. When the rain and wind finally came, the big drops bounced on the surface of the water. I switched back to the old reliable Midget Spinner in the silver-glitter finish. Before the rain, it had seemed impossible to beg, borrow, or steal a strike. Suddenly it seemed impossible to make a cast without receiving one. Maybe it was added oxygen. Maybe it was a sudden lowering of the water temperature. At any rate, instead of being lethargic, the bass turned vicious. One after another struck. I returned them all to the river.

I had figured out that about one out of every twenty-five strikes came from a big bass. That meant that if you did not connect and produce when the opportunity arrived, you had to wait on the average for two dozen more strikes to occur until there was action from another big one. We called the big ones hams because they looked like Virginia hams when they jumped out of the water while being played.

Now the strikes were coming with such regularity that I thought I was due for a big one. Finally it happened. After the four-pounder was landed, I was ready to call it a day and get out of the chill of the driving rain and wind.

The Phillips Tackle Company of Alexandria, Pennsylvania, markets the handsome and effective Midget Killer, a two-prop lure, and Joe Farcht, of Mount Wolf, Pennsylvania, produces the Little Joe, a fine one-propeller lure.

In recent years the L. & S. Bait Company has made available a sinking propeller plug called the Mirrolure that features a bright and flashing scale finish.

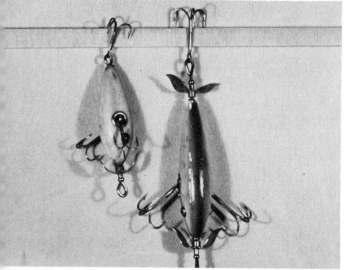

DOWAGIAC
by James Heddon Co.

The firm of James Heddon, soon to become James Heddon's Sons, produced an amazing series of lures. Number two on the hit parade was a sinker. Jim must have been exceedingly loyal to his Michigan hometown, for he chose to name this lure also *Dowagiac*. It was produced in two sizes, as illustrated. The two favorite finishes were rainbow and crackle-back. It was advertised in the 1915 William Mills & Son Catalog.

LITTLE GEORGE
by Tom Mann's Bait Co. of Eufaula, Alabama.

Little George was designed to sink fast and fish deep. It is frequently fished in submerged timber by up-and-down jigging.

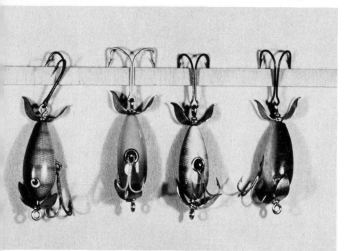

MIDGET SPINNER
by the Shakespeare Co.

Had this lure of the mid-30s enjoyed the reputation and popularity around the land as it did up and down Pennsylvania's Susquehanna and Allegheny Rivers, it would have been king among lures. This sinker was a perfect balance between weight and depth on the retrieve, bulk and pulling power on the cast—a great antique.

MIRROLURE
by L & S Bait Co.

This lure possesses the brightest possible flashing finish.

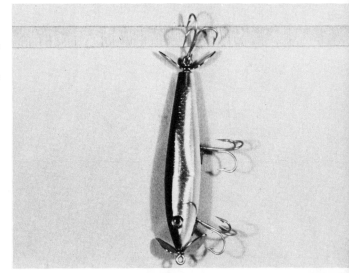

SINKING PROPELLER LURE
by James Heddon Co.

When Heddon produced this model their thoughts were on realistic form and the smaller salt-water fish.

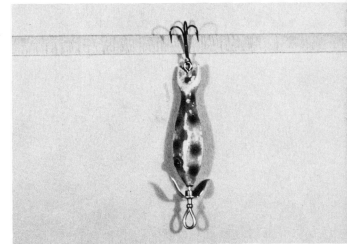

SINKING PROPELLER PLUGS
homemade by Charles Fox.

These plugs were made when there were no available ¼-oz. lures. They were specifically for light-lure bait casting.

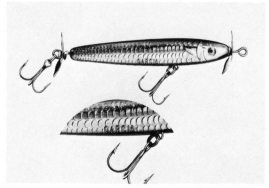

TOM CAT
by Garcia.
This flashing and scaly lure is a fine cloudy-water attraction.

VIBRATING PROPELLER LURES
homemade by Bob Bates.
These sinking propeller lures vibrate as the props rotate at different speeds. One end of the blade is long and trim and the other end is short and wide, but the holes are drilled at the balance points.

WEIGHTED WOODEN LURES
in different versions.
A bevy of sinking underwater propeller plugs of the final years of the weighted wooden lure. These plugs accounted for some superb bass catches, particularly of river smallmouths.

To my way of thinking, the two best-producing lures for large-mouths in lakes and farm ponds both fall into the weighted-fly-and-spinner category, yet they are not similar in looks or principle. Unfortunately, both are now antiques, not because they were not effective in many hands and popular with many anglers, but because they were intricate, each requiring fly-tying and other handwork that makes them too expensive to produce nowadays.

Look at the business of lure manufacturing in this light. The producer has his team of manufacturer's representatives who take orders from jobbers and the purchasers for chain stores. The jobber in turn has his own team selling to dealers. The dealer sells over the counter to the anglers. In order to realize a profit and remain in business the manufacturer must establish a list price on his product that is five times greater than the unit cost. I do not see how the great old Minno-Bug could be produced in this day and age for less than 75¢ each. With the five-to-one markup, this would set a list price at $3.75, and that would create an impossible situation. But how about the lure-making hobbyist? That is a different matter.

At the time in the 20s when a sort of belly dance called the shimmy was the teenage vogue, Al Foss was the national champion tournament caster. This inveterate angler got the idea that what was needed in a lure was a combination of compactness, small size, vibration, and flash. He placed on the market three lures to which pork rind could be attached, each having a new-type propeller on the front. Two of these were just another two lures, but the third, which he named the Shimmy Wiggler, was for years a giant in the field. These lures were manufactured and distributed by the American Fork and

Weighted Hair, Feather-Skirt, and Spinner Combinations

See picture section beginning on page 64

Hoe Company, the producer of golf clubs and the then famous True Temper tubular-steel rods.

The Shimmy Wiggler incorporated a flat metal body with a keel attached by a screw, a bucktail attached to a single hook, and a button for pork rind. The blade made the lure vibrate, and this made the bucktail breathe. It is my estimate that for a time this was the best-selling lure and the greatest fish producer. Incidentally, it was packaged in a small tin box.

Back in 1951 I published a book about lure fishing for bass which was dedicated to the memory of an old hunting and fishing companion who passed on to his reward while hunting in British Columbia. Elmer Lower started his lure-fishing career for bass with an amazing experience. He had an outfit I had selected for him right down to the Shimmy Wiggler. The scene of his initial plugging experience was the middle of the Susquehanna, less than a mile from the eating and drinking emporium he operated in the wonderful town of New Cumberland. While undergoing the trials and tribulations of a beginner with a bait-casting outfit, he managed to cast well enough to a grass patch to be rewarded with a strike. The smallmouth bass that struck was hooked, played, and landed. It was a heavy twenty-two-and-a-half-incher in the six-pound class, the largest smallmouth he was ever to catch.

I'd like to talk now about what I regard to be the best made, most beautiful, and most effective sinking lure ever produced by the hand of man. It came from Sunshine Ranch, San Antonio, Texas, where Robert McGarrough produced his hair and feather bedecked weighted spinner. When the creator of Mack's Minno-Bug was drowned in a canoe accident in South America, the last of his wonderous lures had already been produced commercially. I still have four of them in the ⅜-ounce size, one being in mint condition, but I hesitate to use them. Would that it were four dozen.

The Minno-Bug is a weighted fly and spinner that lands with a flat smack instead of a stony plunk. The spinner is a good one of the Junebug type, the metal head is beautifully painted with big eyes, and the single hook is dressed with a combination bucktail and streamer fly. The bucktail was closely clipped near the hook eye, thus forming a neat collar around the streamer hackles. The creator of the Minno-Bug used wire instead of tying silk to dress the fly, probably so the hair could be pulled harder and packed tighter. There was a special hidden loop for the attachment of pork rind, if the angler should choose to use it, and an ingenious detachable weed guard.

The Minno-Bug has several times brought me outstanding catches of bigmouth bass, the never-to-be-forgotten kind of thing, under very adverse conditions. Two of these occasions were at muddy ponds, in waters that were continually roiled by carp. The third took place on a clear lake laden with aquatic vegetation. The first catch was made on the Black Prince Minno-Bug; the second on the Imp, a yellow and black combination. The clear-water catch was accomplished with a Yellow Sally Minno-Bug equipped with a brass-colored spinner blade, the other blades having a nickel exterior and a red interior. The choice of color combinations was wide.

The two muddy-water catches were similar in four respects: It was the first time I had fished either place; the water was so muddy I was disappointed and discouraged; after each cast the lure was permitted to sink to the bottom then retrieved slowly and deep; and in both incidents strikes were plentiful and the bass were big. This same technique with the same lure has worked well for me on the bigmouth bass of the rich, cloudy fertilized farm ponds, which for me have been the most difficult of all bass waters.

The clear-water catch was made in a two-hour period one early July evening on a pond known as Strack's Dam. This artificial lake in the Pennsylvania Dutch country is the property of the fishermen, that is, the Pennsylvania Fish Commission has purchased it.

That evening all the boats had been rented or borrowed, and there were fishermen along the shoreline. It was difficult to find a free area to fish. Midway along one side of the lake was a dense bed of submerged elodea that jutted out into the lake about 135 feet. From the relatively flat bank it was possible to cast beyond this point and retrieve the lure parallel to the weed bed. Both sides of the weed bed could be fished in this manner. It was a good-looking setup, and strangely there was no boat at the apex of the triangular weed bed and not a fisherman along the bank at this point. Even as I fastened the Yellow Sally Minno-Bug to the monofilament I saw a commotion right where the first cast was to go and was not too surprised when the cast was rewarded with a fish.

Several minutes later I took a three-pounder, and then in quich succession three more, all over eighteen inches. Half a dozen fishermen several of whom had probably never made a cast in their lives, wanted to buy the little lure.

Three other lures in the weighted-fly-and-spinner category are Weber's Twin Buck, the Heddon Queen, and the obsolete Shannon Twin Spinner.

BASSBALL
homemade by Don Dubois.

Don DuBois, of trout fame, and this author combined efforts to make this different type of surface lure. The spinner, designed and patented by Don, continuously reverses direction. It is set between a sphere and a bucktail-laden treble hook to produce unique action for night fishing for big bass and daytime, choppy water surface fishing for muskies.

BUSH DEMON
by Bain Mfg. Co. of Grenada, Mississippi.

There are many small manufacturers of lures, particularly in the Midsouth, and all, it seems, produce three types of lures: spinner baits, jigs, and plastic worms. The spinner bait of today is basically a combination of *Shannon Twin Spinner* and *Mack's Minno-Bug*. Note the *Bush Demon's* double spinner blades and double tail material.

AL FOSS DIXIE WIGGLER
by the American Fork and Hoe Co.

In 1923 Al Foss designed this as a companion piece for his *Shimmy Wiggler*.

FLICKER SPINNER or RATTLER
by Marathon.

This lure features the combination of a metal wobbler with fluttering willow-leaf trailers.

HAWAIIAN WIGGLER
by Fred Arbogast.

Fred Arbogast introduced the *Hawaiian Wiggler* with the *Hula Popper* skirt. This was the forerunner of the southern "spinner bait."

HOSS
by Four Rivers Tackle Co.

This lure has a hammered metal spinner and a combination colored plastic and dyed hair body. Note the ingenious use of a rubber band for weed guard.

MACK'S MINNO-BUG
by the Sunshine Ranch.

Mack McGarrough of Sunshine Ranch, San Antonio, Texas, placed on the market the most elaborate lure of all and one of the all-time greats. The death of its maker in a canoe accident also ended the life of this superb "spinner bait," which came in three sizes and twelve beautiful patterns. Had Mack lived, it is doubtful if his *Minno-Bug* could have survived the era of low unit cost and large discount.

Mack's Minno-Bug was so well made and worked so perfectly that it's certain that its creator spent much time in trial-and-error experimentation to perfect it. Pictured is the naked body. A mold can be made to form such a body. Several simple steps follow. See illustrations for making this lure, on page 220.

MACK'S MINNO-BUG
homemade by Wayne Long.
See page 220 for construction details.

MONKEY SPINNER BAIT
by Bain
has legs and a gold hook.

NO TANGLE SPINNER
by Lou Eppinger.

A 1972 creation, has a bent shaft, and the decorated treble hook is interchangeable.

ORIENTAL WIGGLER
by American Fork and Hoe Co.

This was designed and sold by Al Foss in the twenties when he was national bait casting champion. With it is a special strip of pork rind which softens and becomes flexible after soaking.

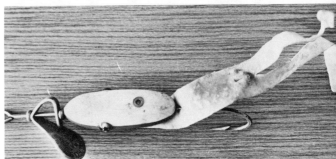

PFLUEGER LUMINOUS TANDEM SPINNER
by Enterprise Manufacturing Co.

When properly weighted, this becomes a highly effective casting rig. In the World War I era it was traditional to decorate the treble hooks with a combination of white and red-dyed chicken feathers and undyed guinea-fowl feathers.

PHILLIPS SPINNER BAIT
by the Phillips Tackle Co.

George Phillips made this great bass lure which had a yellow bucktail on the treble hook.

SHANNON TWIN SPINNER
by the Shannon Lure Co.
This *Shannon Twin Spinner* #2 of the twenties was built and tied around the Jamison barbless hook. It was the forerunner of all the so-called spinner baits of today.

SHIMMY SPINNER
by the American Fork and Hoe Co.
In the early days of spinning in America, True Temper placed on the market this new and smaller edition of the famous *Al Foss Shimmy Wiggler*. The estimated year of its introduction was 1949.

AL FOSS SHIMMY WIGGLER
below, by the American Fork and Hoe Co.
It was fitting and proper that the National Casting Champion, Al Foss, would design and produce his idea of a bass catcher. This was known as a "pork rind rig," but it was frequently fished without the rind. The patent date was 1918. During the 20s this may have been the most catching lure of both fish and fishermen. It was produced in three sizes and in brass and nickle with a variety of bucktail colors. This great lure had five parts: there was a sensitive, well-designed spinner blade, a flat top plate, a thick keel, and a bucktail-dressed single hook. The fifth part, a screw, locked together the components. It was packaged in a small tin box.

SPIN FIN
by James Heddon's Sons
is a deluxe spinner bait.

STRIKE KING
by Sampo, Memphis, Tenn.,
has a ball bearing swivel and a rubber skirt.

TWIN BUCK
by Weber Lifelike Fly Co.
This ingenious lure casts and fishes extremely well. In this case, the tightly revolving willow-leaf blades spin beside the bucktail-decorated single hook. The lure operates the same with either side up.

TWIN SPINNER
by James Heddon's Sons.
The Heddon variation of the *Shannon Twin Spinner* is well constructed and properly weighted.

VEE'S DEVIL
by Vee of Huntingdon, Pennsylvania,
features a willow-leaf spinner, which reduces drag for the retrieving fingers, and dyed hair.

WOOLLY BULLY
by Tom Mann's Bait Co.
Tom Mann, ex-warden, is a guide at Eufaula, Alabama. This spinner bait has a plastic body with a wiggly tail.

Back in the 20s everyone who trolled for muskies and pike had more than a nodding acquaintance with three particular spoons, one produced by Skinner and the other two by Pflueger.

Casting Spoons

The Skinner Spoon was a fluted blade on a sturdy shaft ahead of a large treble hook decorated with red, white, and guinea feathers. The fact that it was the favorite lure of two angling patriarchs of another generation speaks well for it. Bill Vogt, a master angler who wrote the book *Bait Casting* and entertained on the stage with casting exhibitions, and Warren O. Smith, who was the fishing editor of *Outdoor Life* and the author of angling· books, would not go forth without their Skinner Spoons.

Every guide knew about the Pflueger Lowe Star and Buffalo baits, which were available in single or double form. Like the Skinner Spoon, they had sturdy shafts and big treble hooks decorated with red, white, and guinea feathers.

See picture section beginning on page 74.

Some years later Pfleuger produced the Muskill Spoon, which featured a blade that had a copper finish with aluminum spots on the outside and a red finish inside. It is fitted with a treble hook heavily dressed with colored bucktail. The weight of the wet hair helps with the casting.

In 1970, when the professional caster Bill Herdesy was a Pflueger vice president, I sent him an SOS for some of the great old spoons, but I was too late. Since then the company has changed hands, however, the new firm still manufactures the great old line of reels in Florida.

These spoons were popular with both trollers and casters, and they had much to do with the growth in popularity of muskie and pike fishing. There are many anglers around the land who are still looking for them, I being one, but manufacturing costs may have dealt a death blow to them, unless the Japanese come through.

The design of a good casting spoon must be much more exacting than the design of a spoon that is to be trolled only. The more rounded the blade, the further it stands out from the shaft when being drawn through the water; the narrower the blade, the closer it rides to the shaft. The resistance offered by the round blade can be very tiring to the reel hand, but the willow-leaf type is not tiring. The round blade can be made easier to reel by the use of a special plate or attachment that holds the blade near the shaft.

Currently, there are two casting spoons being produced specifically for pike and muskies. The Black Panther was designed by (?) Miller, of Huntington, Pennsylvania, specifically for muskies in the pool where the Raystown Branch enters the main Juniata River, and it has produced well on the grown-up muskies that were planted there as fingerlings. The other is the Giant Killer, a member of the extensive Mepps family. It's a willow-leaf spoon ahead of a treble hook well decorated with bucktail and streamers, the whole being compact and castable.

Miles Weaver, of Kutztown, Pennsylvania, has designed, tested, and refined the Grabber family of high-quality spinner lures that are suitable for casting to all game fish. Both size range and pattern range are extensive. The special treatment of the metal blades produces much color and flash, and the dyed squirrel tail on the treble hooks is beautiful and different. A second series in the Grabber family employs a spoon ahead of a well-painted rubber minnow. This high quality line is now produced and distributed by Bob McGuiney of Kempton, Pennsylvania.

The revolving spoons were predated by the nonrevolving shoehorn wabblers. Tradition has it that a table spoon was accidentally dropped overboard, and as it twisted and flashed to the bottom, it was hit by a pike. It is sometimes said that this incident took place on Lake Bomoseen, Vermont. This gave Julio Buel the idea of creating a lure that would look and act like the spoon being drawn through the water.

Lou Eppinger marketed his idea of a spoon hook, calling it the Dardevle. Eventually it became available in a variety of sizes and colors, with either attached single hook or trailing undressed treble hook. The red and white striped finish on the convex side and nickle or copper finish on the concave part became renowned. Many a pike and walleye have been caught on Eppinger products. The Dardevle Imp, with its attached single hook decorated with bucktail and streamer fly has been good to me, particularly when fished deep and slow for walleyes. All versions of the Dardevle must be used with a snap swivel, to prevent the line from twisting and to keep the edge of the attachment ring from cutting the knot.

The next popular spoon to come along was Johnson's Silver Minnow, which in spite of its name has been produced in gold and in black finishes as well as in silver. This spoon, used in conjunction with pork rind or pork chuck, has developed a reputation for Florida bigmouths.

When Tony Accetta was national professional casting champion, he placed on the market through the Shakespeare Company a nickle spoon equipped with a propeller on the front and a single hook dressed with bucktail on the rear.

There are some new spoons of the attached single-hook variety available now with handsome prismatic finishes. Some were displayed at the great 1972 sporting goods show in Chicago, where they were introduced by the B. F. Gladding Company.

As a rabid muskie fisherman, I hope to see the day when there will again be available a version of the great old revolving-spoon on a shaft with a treble hook heavily dressed with bucktail that quivers and breathes but doesn't rotate, the whole thing weighing in at about ¾ ounce. If it is not practical for a North American manufacturer to produce such a lure, maybe some enterprising Japanese firm can.

Classification of Lures

ANTIQUE SPOONS
by maker or makers unknown.
These antique spoons of unusual design were collected and given to the author by Bill Czapp, an expert crappie and bass angler.

COPPER DELANEY
by an unknown maker.
Before World War I, the famous trolling spoon for Susquehanna River walleyes, which were locally called "salmon," was the *Cooper Delaney*. It was used in conjunction with a single hook baited with a lamprey eel or night crawlers.

DARDEVLE
series by Lou Eppinger.
Lou Eppinger, with his *Dardevle* series in many sizes and color combinations, became famous as the manufacturer of the wobbling spoon of the shoehorn type.

DARDEVLE SPOON
by Eppinger in different versions.
If a strip of pork rind is to be added to a *Dardevle* with a treble hook, it should be attached to the hook prong that falls in the middle, in order to retain balanced action.

DARDEVLET and DARDEVLE IMP
by Lou Eppinger
have single attached hooks decorated with fur or feathers and stiff wire weedguards. All Eppinger lures have little air resistance and have great pulling power.

WINGED DARDEVLE IMP
by Lou Eppinger.
The late Lou Eppinger experimented at length to perfect his three-hook-point *Winged Dardevle Imp.* This ingenious spoon hook has an excellent record.

GIANT KILLER
by Mepps.
Its willow-leaf blade is easy to retrieve, and the bucktail on the treble hook breathes. A fine muskie and pike lure.

MARATHON SPOON
two versions by Wright and McGill.

METAL WOBBLER
by the South Bend Bait Co.
The well-made old South Bend *Metal Wobbler* in the black and white silver flash finish was a great one on chain pickerel.

PEARL WOBBLER
by an unknown maker.
The difficult-to-cast *Pearl Wobbler* goes back to the 20s, when it gained a reputation as a trolling lure for lake trout. Used with copper line, solid or braided, it could be held at the desired depth, which was way down.

PFLUEGER CHUM
by the Enterprise Manufacturing Co.
was a well-designed and fine-casting spoon-hook.

PFLEUGER MUSKILL SPOON
by the Enterprise Manufacturing Co.
In the world of casting and trolling spoons the Pfluegers of the old Enterprise Manufacturing Co., of Akron, Ohio, held a place comparable to that of Heddon in the world of the casting plug. Both the *Lowe Star Spinner* and the *Buffalo Baits* were renowned. The pictured *Muskill Spoon*, is heavy enough to cast with muskie and pike tackle but is not uncomfortable to retrieve. Many muskie and pike fishermen were distressed to learn of the end of the supply of this and other Pflueger blades, which passed out of the picture in 1971 when Pflueger left Akron.

RED EYE WIGGLER
by Hofschneider of Rochester, N.Y.,
is a highly effective wobbler made to cast well.

SONAR
by James Heddon's Sons.
This tricky sonic lure is a violent vibrator.

SPIN DODGER
by Tony Accetta.
When Tony Accetta was the professional casting champion he designed this casting spoon for Shakespeare. It encompassed various features, including a good head spinner and attached single hook with weedguard and hair. As would be expected, it lent itself to good casting.

SPOONPLUG
by Norwoods Tackle Co. of Milwaukee, Wis.,
can be cast or trolled. The story has it that when this unique lure was written up in *Sports Illustrated*, the demand for it became so great that its creator and manufacturer had to employ sixty additional people to supply the market.

SPOON LURES
one a weedless lure by Lou Eppinger.
Julio Buell is credited as being the inventor of a spoon for fishing after he watched a pike strike a sinking and fluttering table spoon accidentally dropped overboard. Whether his pilot model was a spinner on a shaft or the shoehorn type is a moot question. Pictured are the two very different types.

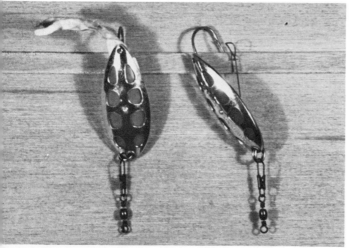

SUN SPOT SPOON
by an unknown maker.

This ingenious lure was not made to cast, nor was it designed to maintain depth, but when attached by means of a snap swivel and with a little flat lead anchored under the single hook, it became a fine spoon-hook for casting.

TRIX ORENO
by the South Bend Bait Co.

This spoon-hook was well made and tricky. The three body components and the hook were held together by three screws, and there was a fluttering tail spinner wired to the single hook.

WEAVER GRABBER
by Bob McQuincy of Kempton, Pa.

This high-quality series comes in three patterns and six sizes. Their creator is an ardent angler, hence his lures have been well tested and are highly practical. Miles Weaver hit upon an amazing treatment of spinner-blade finish, while is not only different but highly effective. These lures come with dyed squirrel tail, painted rubber minnow, or naked treble hook, and their usefulness ranges from mountain brook trout to giant lake trout and all else in between.

If it is not accurate to say that the plastic worm originated in the great reservoir country of the Midsouth, there is no question that this is where it was developed into a renowned bass catcher. Fishing the plastic worm has been refined to an exacting degree, and it is so effective on big-water school bass that its use is universal in the bass-catching tournaments. In fact, were it not for this new and different casting lure, the fishing competitions and the bass clubs might never have come into existence, and without them there would have been no bass-fishing TV shows.

The early plastic worms and eels were hooked into a jig so they could be cast farther and would sink faster. Then came some metal-keel contraptions that were designed to make the single hook semiweedless. There followed arrangements featuring a propeller, glass beads, and gold single hooks in tandem formation.

In the early stages of its development the plastic worm was intended to be a deceiver, to have the nightcrawler look. Then came the attractor concept. The many size variations and color phases probably made selection by the angler more complicated than it was for the bass. Purple, of all colors, emerged as the popular favorite, with black as runner-up.

Once tournament champions were crowned, there followed sponsored bass-catching TV programs featuring the money winners. For the first time the fishermen away from the South saw how it is done. Suddenly plastic-worm fishing became standardized and widely popular.

The standard rig employs a large single hook, usually size 2 or 2/0, of the fine bronze-wire variety. The point of the hook is pushed straight down the nose of the worm for about three quarters of an inch, then brought out through the neck. The worm is tucked up the hook shank to the hook eye. The hook is

Plastic Worms

See picture section beginning on page 81.

then turned around and the point, including the barb, is inserted into the worm, making the hook weedless. The next step is to place a ⅜- or ½-ounce slip-on sinker on the monofilament. This sinker is football-shaped or pear-shaped with a hole running laterally through it. The last step is to tie the "baited hook" to the weighted monofilament with a good knot, such as the Major Turle connection. Now the angler is ready to go to work with his weedless plastic worm.

The idea is to fish the worm where a school of bass is likely to be. Much of this fishing is done in about twenty feet of water· that is adjacent to cover. In impoundments, prime spots are at former stream channels, at submerged bridges or buildings, and near submerged trees or other cover.

The weedless rig is cast and the sinker is permitted to pull it to the bottom. The worm is jerked so that it jumps, then when it has settled down it is drawn slowly along the bottom, now and then being given a mild jerk. When the rod tip is held high, it is sensitive to any tug or tap, so a fish taking the worm is immediately felt.

The angler's strike must be sharp and hard because the hook must not only be sunk in the bass, it must first be driven through the plastic worm.

One acquaintance of mine takes an annual muskie fishing trip to the Elephant Lake sector of Ontario. When he wants to take things easy but doesn't want to stop fishing, he drifts an oversize worm, a snake, really, rigged for muskies. This technique has been good for a few strikes each trip and was responsible for a wild story about a big one that got away.

The plastic worm in various ramifications is here to stay. Its most effective use will be in lakes where the big bass rest in deep water by day. In no way is it supposed to take the place of the various other types of lures, but it certainly has its own special place.

The late Al Reinfelder, former Florida guide and sales manager of the Garcia Corporation, experimented at length with the rubber worm before putting his idea of a really good one on the market, and a Texas lure-maker named Nick Creame combines special jigs to which either very short or long rubber worms can be attached.

Bill Plummer, premier New England bass fisherman and big-fish specialist, has popularized cool-water bass fishing. He has designed a special rubber lure to be fished in jerks, slow and deep, mainly in the late fall. He calls it the Water Demon.

A kindred lure is the pork-rind eel. There is a hinged plastic version of this with a transparent plastic lip. I met a youth who had used this lure to catch numerous bass and pike and two muskies from Summerset Lake at the town of Summerset, Pennsylvania, while fishing during the heat of summer. Incidentally, the muskies and some of the bass were taken at night, but such was not the case with the northern pike.

As this is being written, a new worm is being placed on the market, this version having a hollow tail that stands upright when all other parts are at rest on the bottom.

All the manufacturers who produce the spinner lures also produce plastic worms and jigs.

ALOU EEL
by Garcia
has a lively yet graceful wiggle.

FLIPTAIL
center, by Steinbridge Products, East Point, Ga.
It became standard operating procedure in worm fishing to bring the hook point down through the head and out the neck then back into the body over the barb. A slip sinker is placed on the monofilament before the tie is made to the eye of the hook. The popular colors became purple and black. The lure is fished mainly on the bottom in deep water, and experience has taught the fishermen, particularly those participating in tournaments, to answer the strike of the bass immediately and with authority. This is the system made public on TV shows by Jerry McGinnis, Gadabout Gaddis, and Virgil Ward.

Classification of Lures

FROG and MUDDLER
by Garcia.
The singlehook *Frog* has very sensitive legs, and the realistic *Muddler* is a good imitation of the freshwater sculpin which is common in cold-water streams.

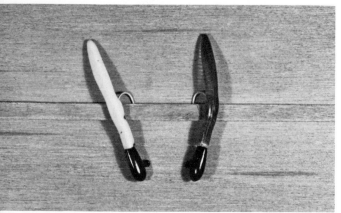

LAZY IKE WORM
by Lazy Ike
combined lip, casting weight, and tandem hooks to create an active casting worm.

PLASTIC GRUB and LEAD-HEAD JIG
by Nick Creme of Tyler, Texas.
Nick Creme has added a short plastic-worm body to his lead-head jig and furnishes an extra worm with each head. Probably the credit for pioneering and promoting plastic-worm fishing should go to him.

PLASTIC WORM
by Nick Creme.
The early standard system was to attach a worm to a naked jig. The lure was permitted to sink to the bottom, then fished slowly. The bass was believed to roll the worm in a ball, then take the head with the hook; so it followed the fisherman delayed his strike. But many a fish dropped the bait and worm fishermen having learned, now strike quickly.

REALISTIC RUBBER LURES
by Burke.

These two are at their best down deep in cold water where the bass have stacked up for the winter.

TANDEM HOOK WORM
by Nick Creme.

The next worm rigs to come on the market were a series of plastic worms equipped with hooks in tandem plus red beads and spinner blades.

WATER DEMON
by Bill Plummer, noted New England bass authority,

is designed for deep-water bottom fishing when it is cold. It is manufactured by Harrison of St. James, New York.

WEEDLESS WORM
by James Heddon's Sons.

The weedless approach by Heddon to plastic-worm fishing.

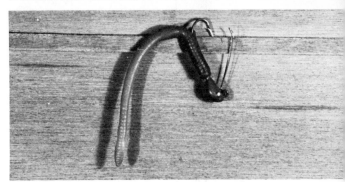

WILD THING
produced by Garcia

is an appropriate name to the late Al Reinfelder's eel.

Jigs

*See picture section
beginning on page 87*

During the early years of my bass fishing, there was no legal fishing for bass in the late fall, winter, and spring. The closed season did not bother the fishermen, since they assumed that this was the hibernation period for bass and that they could not be caught during this time. I felt sure they hibernated, because one time while wading across a bass stream during a February red-fox chase I stumbled onto a piece of stove pipe. Because it was an ugly piece of junk, I raised it with my foot and started to lift it from the stream. Much to my surprise two fifteen-inch bass slipped out of it. They were so torpid with cold that they appeared to be in a state of hibernation, so I stuffed them back in their pipe and put it back in the stream.

Eventually the bass season was changed so that it was closed only during the spawning season. When this change was made, a possible new trail became visible to Ed Crumlick. Now, Ed Crumlick is the most rabid river fisherman one could ever expect to meet. He is his own boss, he is a superb fishing analyst, and he makes some of his own lures.

Ed and I are now friends, but before we ever saw each other I had seen his picture in the paper and had read about him. The story had it that he was catching winter bass in high cloudy river water on homemade jigs. Up till then I had never heard of catching bass in the winter, and the only lures of this type I had heard of were the "Japanese feather jigs" made for surf casting.

Some years later, after Ed had developed a tremendous reputation for bass and muskie catching, he took a mutual friend fishing. Harry Alleman was the MC of a great outdoor TV show sponsored by a conservation-minded manufacturer, and he and Ed got together on the Susquehanna to photograph and tape a show.

After the show had been made but before it was shown,

Harry and I had a conversation. "It got a little cold in the boat," Harry said, "but we were catching bass so fast we didn't notice it. Ed uses two little jigs, one on a dropper. Five times that afternoon he landed doubles. Two of the fish were over four pounds apiece. He told me in advance it would be about like that if he could pick the time."

In due course the program was televised, and I watched it. The film was good and clear. Across the river in the distance was the big tank in Steelton, so I knew precisely where they were. I had kept a boat at a landing nearby and had often fished that very spot in the great limestone ledges. Ed's angling companion, Bruce Middlekoff, was fishing with him while Harry operated the camera. The picture told the story. Each angler cast his pair of little jigs and permitted them to sink to the bottom, then worked them ever so slowly, now and then lifting the rod tip. A lot of bass were caught that afternoon. Thus it was I learned the details of a fishing method that I had not previously even known to exist.

I do not know whether Ed Crumlick was the first to draw and make crawl and hop a pair of jigs in the places where bass stack up for the winter, but I would bet he worked out the system for himself.

When the water is very cold, a bass cannot give his best in the way of a fight, but that does not mean that winter fishing is not enjoyable. When the water is cold, the bass may be too stiff to jump and run, but it's fun nevertheless to be out and after them. I would say that the greatest difference between winter and summer bass fishing lies in what and where they strike. Winter casting is stereotyped in form and limited to special areas, and that is anything but the case with summer casting.

Jigs have their greatest use when the water is cold and the bass are deep and sluggish. That is the time when I concentrate all my fishing efforts on muskies. However, there is another special purpose and special situation where the jig reigns supreme, so let's formulate a hypothetical case to illustrate the point.

It is a summer noon, and a bright sun has sent the bass from the shallows and into shaded places in deeper water. Early that morning we have moved some fish with surface plugs in the pads and also with the skim-and-swim method along the shoreline, but now a strike is hard to come by.

You inform me that what we are doing has become hopeless, to which I agree. Then you say that you would like to try a jig at a shaded dropoff, so we move accordingly. The chosen site is by a sloping wooded hillside.

I row the boat very slowly about 75 feet from the shore and parallel to it. You cast the jig close in to the bank and start the retrieve, then stop it and jerk the rod back, making the lure leap forward then settle down deeper than it was before. This is repeated for about half of the retrieve, then the jig is quickly recovered for the next cast. In this manner the lure is shown to the fish right at the depth where they are located, the dropoff being well covered. But suppose the bass are discovered to be down only about six feet. They might then be reached with a Bomber or a Hellbender or a Go-Deeper River Runt. My experience has been that bigger bass are more prone to hit the plug-type lure. Thus the jig can be used as a fish finder.

The most popular colors in bass jigs are yellow or white hair with a red head. But I know one group that swears by purple jigs, particularly for walleyes, and another great angler I know, Lee Diehl, a Maryland school teacher, likes an all-brown jig.

Somewhere along the line some fisherman said, "Had I been a bottle baby, I would have fished in the formula." As for me, had I been a bottle baby, I would have cast a lure into it.

For awhile during the Great Depression of the 30s I fished every day, all day long, dividing the time between fly fishing for trout and lure casting for bass, both trout and bass waters being close to home. Since then, in the job-holding era, I have been basically an after-dinner angler. Vacation time means a trip to the North woods. Over the years it has been interesting to try many lures on various species and to fish in many localities, but nowadays I have slipped into the habit of concentrating on the local top cream. So that we understand each other, it should be stated that Fox is basically an evening, target fisherman in shallow water, where he hopes turbidity will be as mild as possible. From the time I get to the water until darkness falls, I move along casting to targets, usually with a skim-and-swim lure. Often I loiter for some nights to fish in a weeded bay in a lake or in the tail of a flat in a stream, searching the water with a surface lure. Furthermore, because there are muskies in my bass waters, I fish for both at once, using equipment geared accordingly and simultaneously thinking muskies and bass.

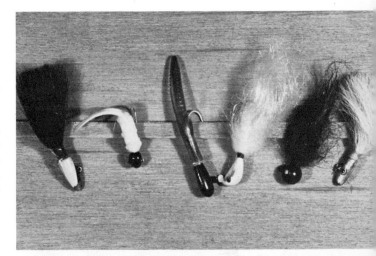

ARCHER JIGS
homemade by Gar Archer.
Liberalization of bass regulations was responsible for a new and different lure as well as a new fishing technique. Northern bass, both largemouths and smallmouths, stack up in winter quarters. The jig is fished slowly and deeply, right in the school. Although bass hooked at this time do not always jump and run well, they still offer outdoor action. Pictured here are some typical jigs.

ARCHER JIGS
homemade by Gar Archer.
The *Archer Jig* was made expressly for winter fishing in the eddies of the Allegheny River of Pennsylvania. The technique is to permit the jig to hit the bottom, then to jerk it hard, and repeat for the entire retrieve. It was on this river that winter jigging was pioneered, and Gar Archer is the recognized father of it. Winter jigging produces both game fish and trash fish, all of which means action.

BLACK BEAR JIG
by Bain.

A use for a jig in the summer is to cast it to the shoreline where there is a dropoff. As the lure is retrieved in jerks it is permitted to sink, thereby sounding until it comes to the level at which the bass are located.

DELWEY BAIN JIGS
by Bain, Grenada, Miss.

These small jigs can be employed at one time, the second one on a dropper from the casting line tied in with a barrel knot a foot or so above the one on the end. Sometimes doubles are caught.

GLIT-R-JIG FLY
by Al Nelson, ⅜-oz.,

is a maribou streamer tied to a weighted sparkling body to give the "fly" pulling power for the lure-casting outfit.

Wonderful Skim and Swim

See picture section beginning on page 102.

An angler shows his quality by what he learns from both the good and the bad, from his successful as well as his unsuccessful experiences. When favorite lures fail, it is time to change a losing game. Furthermore, a seasoned angler knows when to forego a pleasure in order to enjoy a greater one. It was the advice of two venerable fishermen that led me to the above conclusions and eased me into a fresh approach to lure fishing. Once I had found a selection of lures that lent themselves admirably to the new method of fishing these men suggested, it became my favorite and most frequent practice.

I cast back now to the days when the two old anglers passed on to me the secret of skim-and-swim lure fishing. Oddly enough, both men bore the name Lincoln. One was Robert Page Lincoln, an outdoor writer who fished mainly in Minnesota and Wisconsin waters and in Ontario's Lake of the Woods, though it was while winter fishing for bass in Florida that he most often used the technique that his local companion called "pop casting." The other was Lincoln Lender, an avid Pennsylvania lure caster. Each in his own way taught me much of what follows.

This method calls for an exacting choice of lure and a specialized and varied retrieve. Consider this: Built into certain

lures that will float at rest is a potential for both enticing surface action, which can be produced by rod-tip manipulation,
and for a realistic underwater swimming action, which can be
produced by a fast retrieve. Thus the angler controls both the
lure's action and its swimming level, and he can alternate the
two on each retrieve. He can skim it or swim it as he chooses.

But there's more to it than that. The lure can be cast into a
difficult spot—target fishing—and there made to loiter while
being fished on the top. If no strike is forthcoming, the lure is
ducked under the surface and brought back quickly and silently
through the less-attractive water, though there's always the
possiblility of a strike during the recovery for another cast.

There is still more. Sometimes a fish will be interested in
the object making a surface commotion but will not hit the lure.
Although he watches, he won't strike. But when the commo-
tion-maker quiets down, dives beneath the surface, and starts to
silently steal away, that is just too provocative, and a strike is
triggered off.

One day I teamed up with an aging fish warden whose
chosen field of endeavor was governed by love of the game.
Lincoln Lender was a dedicated stream fisherman for "bass and
pike" (smallmouths and pickerel). We were on a favorite
stream of his in central Pennsylvania, the Tuscarora Creek, a
sizeable feeder to the Juniata River. He was the first and last
one-plug fisherman I ever met, the lure being an inexpensive
nondescript whose life expectancy on the market was destined
to be brief.

I looked at the thing as it dangled from the tip of his short
rod. It had a cut-out mouth that looked like the open curved
beak of a bird. This gave the floater a built-in underwater
wabble, Linc explained. He referred to the lure as "my Carter's
Black Joe," and added, "I use it for both bass and pike." Although its finish was battered and peeling, it had originally
been a shiny coal black. It had probably been the first ebony
lure ever marketed. Had Linc not enjoyed a local fish-catching
reputation, I would have felt sorry for him and would have
offered him the use of my lures.

I watched his floater after it landed in the smooth tail water of a long flat. Very slowly he reeled it in, so slowly that it rolled and flopped on the placid surface, but when the retrieve was about half completed, he abruptly intensified the reeling and the lure submerged and wabbled back under water like a crayfish.

When he told me it was the only lure he used and the only way he fished, I should have recognized some new possibilities, but I didn't. We both caught fish that day, but he did much better than I in both size and number, and then I had to take notice.

The day's fishing had a rousing finale. "I want to walk up to that big brush pile," said Linc as he pointed, "and try for an old friend. There's a pike under there that's a two-footer." I went along as a spectator.

The "Carter" hit the water a yard out from the upstream side of the middle of the log jam. On the retrieve it lolled lazily from side to side. There was no popping, gurgling, splashing, or spluttering, just a slow flip-flop, flip-flop, flip-flop.

Beauty is in the eye of the beholder. The explosion that suddenly occurred was a beauteous thing for an angler to behold. Flashing in the eruption under the clobbered plug was a blob of green-gold, not the bass color that I was so familiar with, but something prettier. Linc hauled back hard and hollered "*Strike,*" somewhat unnecessarily, I thought.

"That pike is going to have to break me up if he wants to get back into that brushpile," Linc said as he leaned back. The spring in the arching bamboo cushioned the strain on the line, and out and away from the tangle of snags came the pickerel, which by force of circumstance changed tactics from trying to bull his way back to cover to jumping wildly out in open water. Three times he came straight out, clearing the surface by a foot or two, and tossing a shower of water. With each jump came a wiggling tackle-testing contortion followed by the noisy splash as the fish fell back on the line. Up till then I had never caught a big pickerel, and as I watched, I thought to myself, a four-pound pickerel does as well as a four-pound river smallmouth, which is saying plenty.

Linc finally forced the tiring fish through some snag-free

water and from thence out on the sloping gravel bank. He strung it up with the one bass we had kept, the best one he had caught, a respectable nineteen-incher, and the handsome pair represented a medley of sport. (Fishermen in stream country measure the size of bass in inches, whereas those in lake country, always think in terms of pounds. Being a trout fisherman as well as a bass and muskie man, I like the former method.) I had been watching a happy angler, the master of a specialized game that he had evolved himself, successfully practicing his art. The year was 1943.

In those days a car could be parked near an isolated part of the Susquehanna River at a point where the river broke directly across a series of limestone ledges, and at low water levels it was possible to wade on the ledges and fish the beautiful deep pocket water above and below.

It became my practice to fish ahead, quartering upstream with a skim-and-swim lure. The plug was worked on the surface with rod-tip manipulation until it was carried by the current past my ledge, at which point it was ducked under the surface and made to swim back in the deeper water parallel to the ledge. In this way I could fish a pool, a rapid, and a flat all in one cast, and I believe that this way of employing the skim-and-swim technique is the best possible way to fish that water.

There was an area well out in the river where, with care, it was possible to wade downstream on a gravel bar to another ledge, then fish one's way back in the opposite direction. The adventure was like a tight rope act in that to slip might mean big trouble.

I don't recommend the following procedure, but every so often circumstances led me to do it. I carried my lures in a chest kit with a thong around the back of my neck. When I slipped off a ledge, I would grab the lure kit with one hand and, holding my rod in the other hand, would roll over on my back and kick my way across the deeper water to the next ledge. I became sufficiently skilled at this so that water did not enter the kit and ruin my cigarettes and matches.

One day I was fishing the ledges at sunset, the golden part of the day. I was about a quarter of the way across the mile-wide river, which meant that it was time to drop down to the next ledge and start back while it was still possible for me to see where to put my feet. At the time I was using an orange Spark Plug with a gold scale and red mouth, a finish the bass and I both like.

I can't be sure whether it is fishing fact or fishing fancy, but I think Sparkie's surface action is at its best when the rod tip is given a series of short, snappy jerks so that the sound it makes is *plip, plip-plip—plip, plip-plip*. Sometimes I find myself talking to it. In fact I had just said, "Don't you think it's about time for something to happen?" when Sparkie stopped talking back and disappeared.

My strike was followed by a power run that snatched the handle of the reel right out of my fingers and gave my knuckles a smart crack. I managed to get my thumb on the real spool before a blacklash occurred. A river smallmouth bass normally jumps well, and this one was no exception. What burst out of the water appeared to be the size of a Virginia ham.

I did not rush matters. Some fifteen minutes later I had him by the lower jaw. I guessed his size at about five pounds and twenty-two inches. As it turned out the fish reached both specifications with something to spare. According to my standards, a fish of that sort is worth risking your welfare to hook.

Nature operates in marvelous and mysterious ways. The behavior of each creature is governed by incalculable generations of adaptation and natural selection. All know what they must do and where and how to do it, although there may have been no previous experience or parental instruction. The special interest of the perplexed angler who is attempting to master lurecraft is a trial-and-error study to determine the most appealing way to elicit from the quarry some powerful pull out of the past that will trigger off a strike.

However, one of my great angling experiences was unexpected, lucky, and spectacular. For the sake of sweet memory for me, and for whatever its usefulness may be to you, here is the story as it happened.

On a calm, bright August evening I took my two children

out for bluegills on Opossum Lake, a relatively new impoundment created for fishing with fishing-license monies. This lake
is seven miles from our home and is located in the beautiful
Cumberland Valley of Pennsylvania. Eight-year-old Chip operated with a long cane pole and a tapered leader a little shorter
than the pole, and thirteen-year-old Susie cast with a six-foot fly
rod. Both used little plastic Burke creations with single hooks
imbedded therein, the two favorites being a small white grub
and a tiny realistic-looking crayfish. The barbs on their hooks
were pinched down so they could easily unhook the fish they
caught. Both kids do well, better, in fact, than any adults I have
watched trying to collect a mess of bluegills.

I didn't go along just for the ride, so I had with me a light-lure plugging outfit consisting of a six-and-a-quarter-foot rod, an antique Gulf multiplying reel, ten-pound-test braided line, a ten-foot monofilament casting trace, and a chest full of bass lures. I can cast farther, more accurately, and with a lower trajectory when using light bait-casting tackle than I can with a fixed-spool reel and willowly spinning rod, though I know it works the opposite way for many people, particularly beginners.

I chose a ¼-ounce Whirlygig in a metallic green finish. So as the kids fished for and caught bluegills, I plugged the weed beds for largemouth bass. They caught fish rapidly, which helped matters considerably.

We were fishing from the eastern bank of the lake at sundown, and there was a strong glare as one looked across the water in the direction of the sun. Ordinarily I would not have been caught that way, but this was the best place for the kids. It was a relief when the sun sank behind the horizon and left a brilliant scarlet and orange afterglow. Seen from our angle, the lake took on the same hues though to a modified degree. The smooth surface and the hills beyond were a gorgeous sight.

I was paying more attention to Nature's pageantry than to the little Whirlygig as it worked its enticing way on the surface part way back, then the rest of the way underwater. Suddenly a great wake surged up behind the point where the lure had to be. I blinked in amazement as the water rolled away. Never before in all my bass, trout, and salmon fishing had I seen anything like it.

With heart in mouth I speeded up the retrieve, then slowed it down, then jiggled and jerked and stopped and started, but the lure's tantalizing course brought no strike. The wake dissipated into a mirrorlike smoothness. Whatever had caused the disturbance had slipped away, and everything but the angler was again composed. No strikes were forthcoming on subsequent casts. That was it, at least for the day.

In 1963 some fingerling muskies had been planted in the lake, and since they had been stocked nothing had been seen of them. That had been five years before. Surely this had to be a

This great Susquehanna River smallmouth, over 22 inches and 5 lbs., was one of the first fish caught on the newly created Spark Plug. It came from the limestone ledge water directly below the point where the Pennsylvania Turnpike Bridge spans the river.

grown-up muskie. So now, in 1968, I knew where there was a big, interesting fish.

I returned several times to show a Whirlygig to this muskie. On one occasion Jim Bashline, of the Pennsylvania Game Commission, was with me, and on another trip Vince Marinaro came along. Both men are renowned fly fishermen, and they were considering the potential of shallow-water fly fishing for muskellunge.

On my next foray I was alone. A long cast was required to reach the spot, but I knew I had covered the distance because there was a little tail wind to give my cast a boost. I had estimated the lair of the fish to be in the dead center of the bay. The Whirlygig sailed through the air on a nice, flat trajectory and landed on its side with a lively sounding spat. I let it rest quietly as the rings from the disturbance widened. A jerk set the twirling head in motion, kicking up a little spray. Suddenly there was an eruption, and I glimpsed a great golden blob. The plug was knocked about two feet in the air. It splashed back and everything quieted down. I fished out that cast and many others, but all remained quiet. So ended the second encounter in a near miss.

The next time I gave the muskie a try I had just returned from a fine salmon-fishing trip. It was October and, according to the books, October is a prime muskie month. So in addition to knowing the precise location of a big muskie, I also had the season going for me.

It's funny how minor matters exert their influence in unexpected ways. I was working in a primitive area on land acquisition for the Pennsylvania Department of Forests and Waters. One day as I was driving home I passed through the Dutch country at lunch time, so I stopped at a restaurant and ordered frankfurters, sauerkraut, and mashed potatoes. The platter was typically big, these people insist upon good food and lots of it. I did it justice.

When I got home, late in the afternoon, I was given to know by my wife that we were having one of my favorites for dinner—frankfurters, sauerkraut, and mashed potatoes.

"Oh, no," I exclaimed. "Twice in a row is too much. I haven't recovered yet from lunch. I'll drive over to the lake and show the Whirlygig to that muskie, then stop for a hamburger and a milkshake at the drive-in by the Dickinson College athletic field."

This time was similar to the first in one respect. After the Whirlygig had been made to splatter on the surface and the underwater retrieve had gotten underway, the big wake swung in behind it. Instead of giving it a jerky action, I kept up a fast, steady, arrogant, challenging retrieve, and my heart began to pound. There was a boil that would fill a washtub and a heavy jolt on the rod. I hauled back to sink the hooks.

What followed was interesting and uncertain. Whirlygig was out of sight in the big mouth, but attached to the end of the ten-pound-test monofilament casting trace was a six-inch strand of twenty-four-pound-test nylon, which is a pretty good resister of teeth, even muskie teeth. Eventually his back broke the surface, and a little later I led him into a shallow bay, then skidded his bulk out of the water and over the flattened grass.

Just then a man showed up and identified himself as the caretaker of the area for the state. He was obviously excited and pleased as he measured the fish and jotted down the details of the catch, which added to my pleasure and excitement. My muskie, if not the first, was one of the first caught in the Cumberland Valley, but it certainly has not been my last.

That night Jim Bashline called to talk over a writing project. I said, "Come around and while you're here I'll show you something."

"You mean—you mean that muskie?" he asked hesitantly.

It was not my lot to marry a girl who draws the birds, picks the ducks and doves, and cleans the fish, so after Jim took several snapshots of the muskie, I rolled up my sleeves and went to work. This sort of thing, we agreed, is the only bad aspect of hunting and fishing.

I always carry five different skim-and-swim lures in the tackle box with me in the boat or in the chest kit when I am wading.

The first to be perfected was the Spark Plug. The year was 1948. I most desperately wanted a floater with a beautiful underwater action that would also have a popping face which would catch water. I wanted it to be smaller than Linc Lender's Old Black Joe. I sold my friend Bob Bates on the idea, and we planned and worked together in his basement workshop. The desired combination was elusive. After much disappointment and frustration we finally came up with what we hoped for. Once a model was available I started to work up a supply in various sizes.

Jordon Ewell, a fellow probation officer, who was not a fisherman, had heard me talk about bass plugs, and when he saw the blisters on my fingers from plug-whittling, he chided me about being burned by hot spark plugs. Thereafter he always called bass plugs "spark plugs," and so it was that a nonfisherman named a lure. The name has stuck, and the lure has become well known around home.

Next followed the intricate Whirlygig. I watched the inventive master craftsmanship of Bob Bates in action as he designed and produced in one short evening his idea of a skim-and-swim lure. He liked the old Ans Decker surface bait, so he set out to produce a lure that was like it but which would also swim underwater. He hit on it right away. Since then we have made many dozens in various sizes for ourselves and for friends, and there has not been the slightest alteration in Bob's pilot model.

This lure eventually came to be known as the Whirlygig. They are so intricate and require so much handwork that it will probably never be practical to produce them commercially. For those interested in homemade models, directions for making them are set forth in Chapter Fifteen.

After I accidentally discovered sizeable muskies within a twelve-minute drive from home, I set out to produce a special muskie skim-and-swim lure. Not a single muskie had risen to a popping Spark Plug, which surprised me because they hit the Whirlygig. It was apparent to me that a lure with bobbing and weaving surface action stirred them up, whereas the plunker-type did not. Furthermore, they jumped at, and over, the gurglers without touching them, and once in a while one clobbered a propeller surface lure when the water was rippled by the wind. What I thought I needed was a top-water bobber and a weaver that was longer than it is possible to make a Whirlygig. I was thinking of big muskies, which should be shown a seven-inch plug. The result was a lure I first referred to as the Sick Sucker, and the name has stuck.

At one time, work in land acquisition activity for the Commonwealth of Pennsylvania placed me in the field near the Green Lane Reservoir, so one Friday afternoon I swung in by way of the lake on my way home. The date was October 10, two days before the closing of this fishing resort for the winter. As usual, my casting equipment was in the car, and there was time for about two hours of fishing.

The big dock had been disassembled and pulled up on the lawn. It seemed inevitable that a muskie had been using this overhead cover as home base, the open question being, was he still there or had he deserted the spot when the winterizing operation took place?

I attached the old reliable Sick Sucker in a yellow finish with green scale and pitched it out where the dock had been. The plug landed with a flat, skidding smack, and by twitching the rod tip, I put the plug into its drunken act on the surface. It followed its inebriated course for about twenty-five feet, and nothing happened, so I ducked it underwater for a fast swim for the remainder of the retrieve.

A flashing torpedolike form arrowed at the plug, which then disappeared, blotted out by toothy jaws. I felt the fish hit, and struck back with authority. There was little or no give, and the rod arched deeply. I let it be known to the fellows who were idly talking on the snack-bar porch that I had hooked a muskie.

A half-minute later the hook lost its hold, and the muskie was gone, though he left a characteristic sign that he'd been there in the form of the four holes his big teeth left in the head of the Sick Sucker.

The unusual thing about the incident was the hooking of a muskie on the first cast. Probably this will never again happen to me, but you can bet it is well remembered and often hoped for.

My last great experience of the 1971 season took place shortly before ice locked up 'Possum Lake. It was one of the greatest fishing thrills I have ever experienced. The sun had just dropped behind the wooded hill, there was no breeze, and the lake was like a giant mirror reflecting sky and treeline. My copper-colored Sick Sucker was waddling back toward me across the surface when in its wake a beautiful rippled V appeared and closed rapidly on the lure.

Suddenly there was the greatest explosion of water I've ever seen a fish make. A massive muskie, the thirty-pound kind, lunged out of the water, pushing a sort of gusher ahead of it, then fell back belly first, just missing the lure and causing a great splash. I did not get that fish or even get a hook into it, but the experience was extraordinarily exciting. Such an incident as this cannot be thought of as a failure. It must be considered a partial success, and it will certainly be long remembered.

For me, the Sick Sucker has been the greatest lure by far for both muskies and pike. About half the strikes have occurred when the lure is going through its surface antics, and most of the rest came shortly after the lure began its silent underwater swimming. Many of these lures have been given away to friends, and the demand has become fierce.

One evening when my work had me located in southwestern Pennsylvania, I took a box of untested Spark Plug blanks to the Youghenny Reservoir to test them before painting them and attaching the hooks and screw eyes. Each in turn was cast and retrieved, so that if there happened to be any duds in the lot they could be weeded out.

I was conscious that a man had walked down the concrete ramp and was quitely watching. Finally he spoke. "I would like to talk to you," he said, "because I see what you are up to. You want a two-way lure, one that fishes on top or underneath. I make my own two-way lure for bass fishing in the Kentucky lakes back home. I want to go up to the car and get one for you."

When he returned he remarked that the hand-painted frog-finish lure he offered me was the best thing he knew of for his fishing. I gave him a handful of unpainted hookless Spark Plugs in return, and we parted company. I am sorry now that I did not get his name and address. As it turned out, his ¼-ounce lure, which I started calling the Kentucky Babe, fishes extremely well.

Ned Smith, the renowned wildlife artist and naturalist, lives within easy striking distance of the Susquehanna and Juniata Rivers, and he is a rabid lure fisherman for river smallmouths. His two favorite lures were a floating double-propeller plug and a sinking double-propeller plug. Then he got the idea of developing one lure that could go both ways, thereby joining the skim-and-swim club with his "Flipper."

Jim Bashline, now a staff writer for *Field and Stream,* fishes with Ned and also fishes with me in my meadow on the Letort. Both of us gave him homemade plugs from time to time, and he came to count on them in his lure fishing for bass, both locally and in Canada. It did not take him long to become a skim-and-swim enthusiast. I even made some big Sick Suckers for him to experiment with on salt-water species. At about the same time, Bruce Brubaker, who was a national and international amateur casting champion and more recently the professional casting champion, caused a stir at a national convention of the Outdoor Writers' Association of America in Florida when he did big things on different salt-water game fish with the muskie Sick Suckers I had given him.

It occurred to Jim that these special lures deserved to be more widely known and that the way to bring this about was to get the skim-and-swim group together and apply to the appropriate state authorities to organize a firm, issue stock, and manufacture and distribute the lures. So we followed the path of Jim Heddon, Fred Arbogast, and Charlie Helin, and the outcome was the Penn Dart Company, the skim-and-swim people. Unfortunately, the Penn Dart Company was short lived.

John Rex, a man who has been responsible for the acquisition of tens of thousands of acres of land for the Commonwealth of Pennsylvania and who knows this field better than anyone else, is also a rabid angler, lure-maker, and fly-tier. His favorite muskie plug is a one-ounce Sick Sucker, which he makes himself. John Rex is the person who attached the names skim-it and swim-it to the method and skim-and-swim to the lures, and both phrases have become a part of the angling vernacular.

So the special family of skim-and-swim homemade lures consists of five lures, each having a special use. I rate them as follows: Spark Plug and Kentucky Babe are superb lures for both largemouths and smallmouths of the lakes; Flipper is the premier stream-smallmouth lure; Sick Sucker is a tremendous muskie and pike lure and potentially a great salt-water lure; and Whirlygig is a very happy compromise when the basses and the pikes are sought after at the same time.

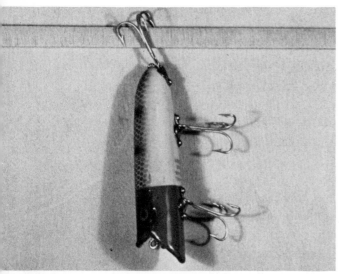

BASSER
by James Heddon Co.
is similar to the *Lucky 13*. Both these lures date back to about 1922.

FLIPPER
homemade by Ned Smith.
Ned Smith, the renowned wildlife artist, makes his own lures and fishes the Susquehanna and Juniata rivers on many evenings. He prefers two-prop plugs, both floaters and sinkers, but he wanted a two-way propeller lure for skim-and-swim fishing, so he designed and made his *Flipper*, which Penn Dart marketed.

KENTUCKY BABE
by the by-gone Penn Dart Co.

This lure combines a popping face with rubber fins to create enticing surface action, and on the underwater retrive it has a fast wiggle. It was hand-made for private use by a Kentucky fisherman for his shoreline fishing for bigmouth bass.

LUCKY 13
by James Heddon Co.

was the first lure that lent itself well to both surface fishing and underwater swimming. Today this combination fishing on a retrieve is known as "skim-and-swim" fishing. The first *Lucky 13*s were made of white cedar and in two sizes.

SICK SUCKER
homemade by Charles Fox.

After considerable trial-and-error experimentation, *Sick Sucker* became the premium muskie lure of Opossum Lake and the Juniata River of Pennsylvania. On the surface it bobs and weaves as it angles from side to side. The swimming action on the fast underwater retrieve is angular in nature at a depth of about eighteen inches. Skim-and-swim fishing lends itself admirably to both muskie and pike fishing. Strikes of big fish on the top are truly explosive.

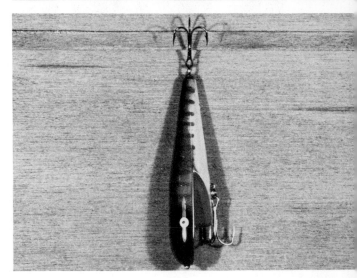

SICK SUCKER
homemade by Charles Fox.
When the monofilament is attached to a screweye on the top of the head of a *Sick Sucker*, the lure swims deeper with wider action.

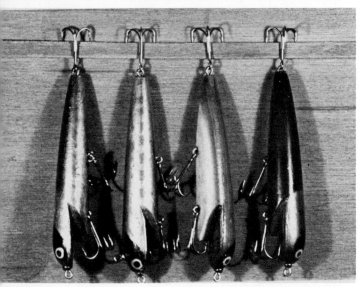

3/4-OZ. SICK SUCKERS
homemade by Charles Fox
are equipped with three sets of treble hooks for muskie fishing.

SUICK SUCKER
by Frank Suick.
Either Frank Suick made the *Suick Sucker* famous or the *Suick Sucker* made Frank Suick famous. This unique muskie lure is fished with violent jerks. Most of the strikes occur after the dive as the lure floats upwards. The Pennsylvania fellows call it the "surfboard."

SPARK PLUGS
homemade by Bob Bates.
The first *Spark Plugs* made in 1948 had a depression ground with a stone in the back of the head, in the belief, which was later revised, that this improved both popping and swimming actions.

SPARK PLUG
homemade by Charles Fox.
Short-lived Penn Dart, the home of the skim-and-swim people, set out to market a series of lures made expressly for skim-and-swim fishing. That is, the lures have built into them excellent surface action under rod-tip manipulation, and at fast reeling they possess attractive underwater swimming action. Thus fish can be shown two different actions at two different levels on any retrieve. In 1948 the author made for himself and some friends a ¼-oz. two-way lure that came to be called *Spark Plug*. It was and is a popper with a fairly wide side-to-side underwater wobble. In the hands of some local casters "Sparky" won a great reputation. The Penn Dart product is hollow plastic, and in addition to being both fine popper and swimmer it possesses pulling power for the best possible casting for its weight.

SPARK PLUGS
homemade by Charles Fox.
A group of homemade *Spark Plugs* ranging in weight from ⅛ oz. to ¾ oz.

SPARK PLUG
homemade by Charles Fox
is equipped with a rubber skirt.

JOINTED SPARK PLUGS
homemade by Charles Fox.
The hinge is made by interlocking screw-eyes.

SURFACE LURE
homemade by Charles Fox.
This lure, which is a *Whirligig* with a propeller at the tail, is strictly a surface bait and a good one for muskies in choppy water as well as for big bass at night.

WHIRLIGIGS
homemade by Charles Fox.
These range in weight from ⅛ oz. to ¾ oz.

WHIRLIGIGS
homemade by Charles Fox.
Whirligig, the great skim-and-swim lure, has proved its worth as the happy compromise when fishing for bass and muskies at the same time. Pictured are ½-oz. lures made by the author for his young son.

WHIRLIGIG
homemade by Charles Fox.
After the unexpected catching of three sizeable Pennsylvania muskies that had been stocked as fingerlings in a five-year-old impoundment, this ¼-oz. green *Whirligig* was retired from service by the author.

Target and Hazard Fishing

Fish do not like bright light, so they are often to be found where the sun casts long shadows. That means that there are along-the-log fish, rock-hiding fish, under-the-bough fish, and fallen-tree fish, as well as lily-pad, spatterdock, and lunge-weed fish. To reach these fish, one must practice the art of target casting, and this presents fascinating complications. It is not stereotyped casting. It takes nerve and skill. The challenge rests in the fact that the greater the hazard of a hangup, the greater the chances for a fish. I ask you, how could one have a more perfect angling situation, a more truly beautiful problem?

The classic approach is one of teamwork between the understanding operator of a comfortable fishing craft and a caster who goes directly for the margin. It is at the edges of cover that the slashing strikes occur. The combination of finesse and a well-chosen lure does the trick. Wherever practical, I like to angle the cast up and ahead of the boat. I think that many fish are made suspicious by the sight and sound of waves from a boat. A cast made a bit up ahead of the craft will very likely increase one's success ratio. However, some spots can only be hit with a straight-in pitch. When two fishermen cast as a third party rows, I would expect the man in the bow to have the better of it, not only because he can work ahead of the boat but also because he will get first chance at fishy spots. A periodic change-about arrangement is in order. And it is more comfortable for a right-handed fisherman to cast ahead from the right side of the boat than it is from the left. Of course the opposite is true for lefties. Operating from a slow-moving craft is more interesting and productive than a fast hit-or-miss approach.

Bass, muskies, and pike do not take lures readily in the depths. Working the shallows is far more productive and that is where the hazards are. Furthermore, weeds do not grow in water over twelve feet deep, and there is little food in the depths. For the lure-caster, the makings of a lake are the shorelines and the bays.

It is not reasonable to expect any game fish to travel through a considerable expanse of warm, shallow water to enter a pad field, but a short trip is something else. The fish will feed where there is an abundance of food, and the pads and other weed beds are full of forage. I have found it interesting to note that, compared with northern pike and chain pickerel, bass and muskies in the pads are suspicious in the extreme.

There are two essential things one must learn to do in pad and weed-bed fishing. The angler must strike the fish fast and hard and then try to railroad it away from trouble as quickly as possible.

Now and then a hook will hang up in the pads or weeds, and it is an abomination to go in with the boat to free the lure. I prefer to use a line strong enough to withstand the strain that's put on it when the lure is torn away from the obstruction or the pad is pulled in. This should be done by hand, not with the rod. This does not destroy chances for a strike in as great a radius as would the invasion of a boat.

The strike to a submerged lure is great, but the strike to the surface lure is terrific. The classic fishing to targets and hazards is to skirt the edge of a pad field, casting into pockets and alleys, and this is very fine, but I wanted to cast right into the pads and retrieve the lure around, over, and among the thickest obstacles, thereby reaching the spots where no one else fished.

I turned to the best lure designer I knew and informed him that we were faced with a challenge—the design and crafting of the Pad Jumper. Here was a case of a lure's being named before being designed. After a couple of tries Bob Bates and I had something that met our two requisites, that is, something that could be cast into the pads without hooking up and that would roll over on its belly when it landed on its back. This lure extracts the battler from the pads.

In 1972 there appeared on the market a lure that I think should give a good account of itself when fished in the pads. Its name is the Bass Charger, made by the Ketchmore Bait Company.

There are certain artificial lakes in Pennsylvania containing muskies where I indulge my proclivity for wading. I like the idea of a lure traveling toward a bank or shoreline instead of away from it. When wading, it is more convenient and less disruptive to release the snagged lure with power rather than to attempt to wade to it. And often it's not possible to wade to a snagged lure. This is the time and the place to be concerned about the integrity of the tackle.

Ron Kommer, a skilled and avid muskie fisherman who makes regular trips to the Kawartha region, fishes one day each week of his trip with an Ontario guide on his day off, which the guide naturally reserves for fishing. The two look for little watery paths that lead through protruding weed beds and into open areas. They say these are the waterways that muskies follow to and from their homes in the limpid depths. Apparently a careful study of muskie ways has disclosed that the comings and goings of the fish keep the muskie trails open.

When these two men fish such places, they carefully move into casting position so that the lure, a Mud Puppy, for instance, can be placed very precisely. In this sort of spot casting one had better believe in each and every cast.

In such situations, the magnificent muskie sometimes shadows the lure before he hits, and when he hits, the strike is a wallowing splash that throws a smother of spray. The angler must then play the muskie to the upper limits of his proficiency as the other man handles of the boat. The idea is to force the muskie over and through the weeds and into open water, where he is played and with luck, ultimately netted.

Shortly before his passing, Bob Lincoln advised me that his favorite fishing was extracting muskies from the pad fields early in the morning, before they desert the area for deeper water.

Conditions may govern the nature of the lure, but the nature of the horsing is pretty much standard. Hauling a fish out and away from the pads may require the mastering of a new technique. When everything works right, the strike elevates the head of the fish, a high rod keeps it up, and fast reeling starts the fish on the way out. The more the fish wiggles and swims, the easier and faster is the railroading, so long as the fish's head is kept high. The longer part of the battle ensues in open water. If things do not go right with the horsing process, the episode was at least a partial success. We should pay tribute to fish that escape. As for the angler, time mellows bitter experience.

Fun can be had in a stump-strewn bay in a bigmouth bass lake, the trick being accurate casting to the shaded sides. Many of the strikes occur when the lure hits the water. To me, that spontaneous surface-smashing reception is the most thrilling strike of all. I attempted to sell the state-parks people in Pennsylvania on the policy of creating bays for hazard fishing in new impoundments by not clearing the land and by making log jams by the use of cables, but because of federal policy and fear of driftwood the idea was considered interesting but unfeasible.

Another interesting type of hazard fishing takes place during high, clear conditions on lakes and rivers when there is a background of bushes and boughs. Maybe it is insects that bring them there, or the presence of crayfish and minnows, but at any rate the bass move in. This makes for interesting target fishing as one casts between, under, and just short of clusters of foliage. Accuracy is the prime requisite.

One need not speculate about the fruitful locations. It does not even take fish sense to find the lurking places. They're obvious, and the object is to cast into them. Inaccuracy creates anything but flattering results. Two totally different lures have worked well for me in such situations.

The first, which in theory seems best, is the Spark Plug, the main thing being to make it look alive when it touches the water, then to stop it and let it rest, before putting it through its paces. If no strike takes place after about five feet of surface action, duck it under for a fast-swimming underwater recovery.

The second great lure for me in this fishing has been the sinking propeller plug, the main thing being to get the action going, that is, to start the retrieve the instant the lure hits the surface. Almost always the strike breaks the surface. Bass lying under the boughs and in the bushes usually attack swiftly.

There is an area of the Susquehanna River below the mouth of the Yellow Breeches Creek known as Hawk Rock, which is the high point of the massive ledges. Today this is known as a muskie hot-spot, but the following incident predates the introduction of muskies in the three-state watershed. It was July, and the big river was high but clear, an unusual combination. Along the sloping bank between the Breeches and the Rock was a considerable growth of scrubby willow with logs and brush piles lodged here and there. Water had backed up under the willows and created floating obstructions out of the debris that had been deposited there by the spring run-off.

I was alone in the boat, and my system was to anchor out from the head and cast a Midget Spinner into the openings, then when satisfied that I'd covered the water, to lift the anchor and drift a little before anchoring again and casting out another little area by the willows and brush. The bass had moved in on this shoreline and were willing to attack. This turned out to be my finest bass fishing for that season, and it took place at a time when some fishermen stayed home because they said there was "too much water."

A comparable incident took place when my Dad and I put up at Blue Sea Lake in Quebec, some sixty-five miles north of Ottawa. I spent most of my time on the small lakes adjacent to big Blue Sea. I prefer the smaller bodies of water where one can shift position easily, and I had found that the average size bass was larger and the pike were much more plentiful in the small lakes.

On this particular year our arrival had been preceded by a siege of rain that increased the level of the lakes two to three feet above normal. The bass had moved under the bushes and were there for the casting. This was back in the 20s, and those were the days of the big plug. We caught some bass but raised many that wouldn't touch the lure. I wonder what might have transpired had they been shown in that clear, shallow water some ¼- and ⅜-ounce lures very accurately delivered.

A more common situation, and one that does not require great accuracy, is to skirt a shrunken shoreline where land and waters blend. Logs, fallen trees, bushes, and rocks that part the surface take on the appearance of great promise, particularly in shallows that harbor both bass and muskies. Here one finds bays, pockets, promontories, and piles of debris, as well as bare or grassy banks from which to jump and drag a lure. Again, this is a place for team effort, with one person casting as the other handles the boat.

In low, clear water I believe in the use of small lures—something of ⅜ ounce or less. A cautious approach is most important. Pitfalls are waves, noise, rowing too fast or too close to the shore, and, most dangerous to success of all, overshooting and sloppy casting.

The most beautiful shoreline I ever saw is in a small but handsome Ontario lake near Bruce Evans's Pine Lodge near Halberton. It abounds with logs, pockets, points, pads, down pines, and overhanging foliage. To make matters particularly interesting, this water presents the combination of bigmouth and smallmouth bass and muskie fishing.

A misconception cost me many wonderful days and some great fish in the part of the Susquehanna below the massive Conowingo Dam, across which U. S. Route 1 passes, in the Maryland part of the big river. When water is released to turn the wheels, the river becomes a raging torrent, from the great pool below the dam to tidewater, where the river widens and deepens into the Chesapeake Bay. When water is being stored and the wheels are not turning, the river recedes, revealing the high sections of ledges. From a distance it appears to be a stony riverbed with no flow and only puddles among rocks, but at a closer range the puddles look more like pools, each with a small flow of water at its head.

The change from one extreme to the other is sudden and frequent. By necessity, the bass will rigidly hold their homes against the flood, then a few brief hours later find themselves in a condition that appears to be the worst possible drouth. It was common talk at Conowingo that fish can be taken only when the wheels are open and that it is useless to fish on Sundays when water is being stored. We fell for this. Finally, for some reason we went down one Sunday to give it a try.

The whole thing looked different once we were in the river. What had appeared at a distance to be puddles turned out to be sizeable pools, many too deep to be waded, with large segments of the ledge protruding, though it was unlike the ledge pocket water we knew so well in the river in the vicinity of New Cumberland.

Our first inclination was to cast into the center of the pools. We were sure that fish were there. Now and then we would spot smallmouth bass and some striped bass up from the Bay. But not everyone studies a problem from the same angle. Why didn't the fish strike a lure delivered to the middle of a pool? Three of the four of us concluded that hearsay was right and the fish don't feed and won't strike when the wheels are closed and the water is low, quiet and clear.

Gene Benner was not sure that we were right. To cast to the shaded side of the protruding rocks turned out to be the distinguishing mark between him and us, between the observant fisherman and the routine casters. In the shade was where they were, and they were not going to move into the brightness to intercept a lure.

At this point the Susquehanna flows, in a general way, from north to south. That means that in the morning the shaded area is on the west side of the protruding rocks and in the afternoon on the east side. Gene had figured out where Conowingo bass reside on low-water Sundays in their struggle for quality living. To catch them in the morning, he waded on the west side of the pools, casting toward the east; in the afternoon, he waded on the east side, casting westward.

That was the solution to half the problem. The other half was the accurate casting of a light lure that produced only a gentle flat smack when it hit the water directly over the fish. In the course of several trips our favorite lures became the Shakespeare Baby Popper and the South Bend Midge Oreno, each of which weigh a mere ¼ ounce. This was in the days before spinning became widespread in America, so we employed balanced bait-casting equipment geared to handle the light lure.

Once we knew what to do, the opportunities to score were great, and the fishing was so good that the four of us went there every Sunday, from the opening day of the season, which was August 1, to cold-weather time.

Occasionally a lure would ricochet off a rock. When this happened, the strike usually came fast upon delivery. In the quiet, shallow pools there would be a tackle-testing surge accompanied by a wake. Once in a while these Conowingo escapades would produce a really big bass.

One day I reluctantly cast into a mess of snags the like of which I had never before attempted. An oak tree, the life smothered out of it years before by a tenacious grape vine, had toppled into a favorite Conodoquinet Creek ledge pocket. What made matters all the more frustrating was the fact that earlier in the season, before the storm blew the tree down, I had located a particularly fine bass in the old reliable hole, which was now covered by a blanket of snags. I tied on my special hazard-fishing lure, a homemade affair. I cringed as the Pad Jumper was on its way to the vine-decked limbs.

The lure landed in the mess and dangled over a runner of the vine. I reeled in ever so gingerly to prevent the swinging plug from wrapping around the vine. It slid up and over the top of the obstruction and dropped to the water, but line was still looped over another part of the vine. Again the lure came up, slithered over the snag, and dropped down. This happened a third time, and then to my relief the lure landed in open water, free of the snag. I made it wiggle and jiggle, then let it rest as the rings widened. Another twitch did it. There was the familiar but always startling eruption. I struck back, and the rod snapped into a throbbing arc.

After the smallmouth jumped, I was able to maneuver it away from its security. When I released the fish it swam in a beeline back to its fortress.

There were two interesting things about this place, which I came to fish periodically. First, the bass that were caught there were taken by hazard fishing in the jam, after casting beside it drew a blank. Second, about half the time the lure did not snag. I concluded that the bass stayed under the debris, out of sight and sound of casts in the open, but that they saw and followed the lure when it was cast into the entanglement and took it when it reached open water.

This tangle gave me my first experience with real hazard fishing, and now I never hesitate to give it a try where the situation calls for it. When a challenge of this sort is met successfully, great personal satisfaction is the reward. All target fishing is interesting, whether the cast be to a pocket in the pads, a grassy bank, a mossy rock, a deadhead, a down tree, or even into a brush pile or log jam.

There is another type of hazard fishing. This is when one retrieves the lure over and through dense weeds protruding above the surface. Bill Aldridge, of the Four Rivers Tackle Company of Greenwood, Mississippi, designed a flat, castable, weedless plastic lure with the express purpose in mind of drawing it over and through weed beds, some of which are draped with algae. Appropriately enough, he calls it the Moss Hopper.

Angler Aldridge warns, "Don't strike back too soon. When you see a disturbance at the lure, give the fish time to break through the weeds and strike the lure. Then you must strike back and railroad the bass out of there." And he adds, "This is real fun, but the tackle must be able to take it."

Insect Influence

If we are to really succeed in our angling, we must capitalize on the opportunities to score as they present themselves. In my judgment, bass fishermen have not paid enough attention to insects. There are times when land-born or aquatic insects are a factor in lure-fishing for bass, just as they are a factor in fly-fishing for trout.

It is an inflexible rule in ichthyology that fish turn to the most readily available food supply for the bulk of their diet. Nature protects the scarce at the expense of the plentiful. There are various insects, both terrestrial and aquatic, that periodically appear in abnormal numbers, and when this happens bass will often feed heavily on them. Nature may have planned that a certain percentage of the diet of bass be composed of crustacea and insects.

It was my great good fortune to have as a house guest on more than one occasion the greatest of all American trout fishermen, a man who devoted his life to angling. The amazing Edward R. Hewitt had this to say about the diet of trout and bass. "Fish as fish food is not nearly as nutritious as either insects or crustacea because fish are lower in fat content. Protein brings about growth and a fish diet has a deficiency of protein.''

An examination of the mouth of a bass clearly demonstrates that it is designed to pick food from the bottom and take it from the surface, then hold and finally swallow the likes of hellgrammites and grasshoppers. The brushlike dental arrangement is totally different from that of the pikes, whose myriad slanting sharp teeth are designed to pierce, mangle, and kill. It appears to me that smallmouths are limited to waters where crayfish abound. In spite of tremendous quantities of bluegills for big-mouth bass to feed on in many farm ponds, these bass do not grow to the great size of those of the lakes, and this may be because of a protein deficiency in the pond.

Each species of insect that bass feed upon has particular places, seasons, and times of day where and when it appears in large numbers. The following insects are all grist for the bronze-back mill: Japanese beetles, winged carpenter ants, grasshoppers, damsel flies, Dobson flies, and the larger aquatic drakes. For the most part, we cannot use a lure to imitate an insect that the bass are feeding on, as we do in trout fishing with a fly, but that is neither necessary nor important with bass.

My first experience with insect-eating bass was remarkable in that the fish were taking something I had never before seen. The setting was the Susquehanna River in Maryland near the mouth of Deer Creek. The time was one hour after daybreak of a mid-July day back in the 30s. On my way back home from Baltimore I stopped at Schweer's landing and cabins. Waking up early the next morning, I decided to go out on the river for a little fishing before breakfast.

I anchored at a ledge not far from a disintegrating bridge pier. Below, the river opened up and slowed down as it merged with Chesapeake Bay. Upstream, the massive ledge formations, worn in irregular patterns by the onslaught of the angry torrent that comes when the gates of Conowingo Dam are open, looked like the skeleton of the earth seen through an open wound. Even though the gates were closed, there were trickles into the pools, mainly from the inflow of Octoraro Creek just below the great dam.

The pools were dotted with rings made by surface-feeding fish, but there was no hatch of flies. Careful scrutiny revealed the reason for the rises. Along the river were some shoulder-high weeds on which Japanese beetles were milling about in the warmth of the early morning sun. Every so often one would start across and drop in the river. Once they were on the water, something promptly took them.

I put on a whittled-down Jersey Wow and cast to a dainty little ring, which looked like the mark a small bass or fallfish might make. There was a slashing, explosive strike, and a fine bass flung his comely proportions into the air and crashed back. It was a sight that never fails to thrill me. When I rolled the hook out of the fish's jaw, there in its mouth was a Japanese beetle, convincing evidence that large bass would take the beetle and sip it with a minimum of commotion.

This was only the start of beetle fishing for me. Time and experience demonstrated that bass rising to beetles would turn from them to lures, displaying no semblance of the selectivity so typical of trout. The lure I have used most on the beetle eaters is the Baby Popper.

On that day I was seventy miles from home, where we had never seen a single Japanese beetle. The reports of their infestation were grave. They were reputed to be terrific defoliators. Doleful gardeners predicated devastation and a fight to the finish between man and pest. There could hardly have been two more dour voices than those of my parents, Mother with her roses and flower shows and Dad with his orchard and other plantings. Trouble was moving our way at the rate of fifty miles a year from a nursery near Riverton, New Jersey, to which the beetles had inadvertently been imported with bulbs and soil from one of the islands of Japan.

The scientific name for this insect is *Popillia japonica*. Now that I have come to know these beautiful, misplaced beetles with the soft-sounding name, I can say things in their favor.

Both trout and bass feed upon them. Strangely, some trout take them in quantity, whereas other trout positively will not touch them. Often I have thrown them into the Letort, a stream that flows by my house, and watched the trout's reactions. The usual time for the beetles to get on the water is shortly after daybreak when they are still stiff and can manage only an unsteady flight.

So far as damage to plants is concerned, they kill nothing, and their food preferences are rather limited. The nymphs start to emerge from the ground about July 1, and the beetle form is seen in quantity for two months. Favorite foods are grape, rose, and plum-tree leaves and, late in their season, button-weed leaves. In addition, they like smart weed, jewel weed, corn silk, and milk-weed blossoms.

By 1940 the beetle was in full residence in the Cumberland Valley. When they drop on the water, the six legs work slowly and methodically. No doubt they put down where they please, not recognizing any difference between land and water. When they fall on bass water, the fish will feed readily upon them, and at such times fishing is especially good. In the digestive process the pepsin in the stomach of the fish dissolves the insides of the beetle, and the empty shell passes through the fish.

One fall I had a great English setter to get into shape for the pending grouse season, and I was training her in the fields on ringnecks and quail. This was a quick, bold dog, and as she worked a field I could see quite a few disturbed insects in flight from her. I managed to catch one, and I'd never seen anything like it. It was obviously of the katydid family, but it was immense, with speckled wings and, of all things, a fat, pink body.

I checked it out with Gene Craighead (of the famous Craighead family of naturalists), a fishing friend in the state Department of Agriculture. Gene told me that it was a rare late-season member of the katydid family. Its numbers are usually kept down by a parasite, but that season they were numerous. When he told me that its mating was done high in the air, I thought of the concentrated lines of drift in the Susquehanna River and what *pièces de résistance* they might be carrying to the bass.

I asked Vince Marinaro, of trout-fishing fame, to go with me to a certain funnel that might feature bass surface feeding on these extraordinary bugs. When we arrived at our destination, the situation was even better than I'd hoped. The giant katydids were there, and the bass were receptive. This insect, we found, propels itself on the water by periodic kicking.

Vince promptly caught a nineteen-inch smallmouth, upon which we performed an autopsy. This bass was so jammed with these insects that when the stomach was cut open they rolled out dry. It was obvious that this fish had taken all he could handle, not letting a single one go by.

I decided that a good surface bait for this occasion would be a Midge Oreno with ends swapped so that the screw eye for the line was in what is normally the tail end. I took several bass with this.

At home that night I fashioned a special lure for this situation. It was made out of walnut and was streamlined and heavy enough to be cast far. Its overall shape was like a little cigar, except that a collar with a concave groove facing forward was located near the back end just about where the insects feet would be in the water. This took some of the katydid-eaters, and it has proved to be a worthy variation of the popper-type surface lure. It can be fished any time a surface bait is indicated.

The most common insect in the world is the ant, which comes in many sizes and colors, but it is only the big carpenter ant that is of interest to catchable-size bass. At mating time the ants develop wings and fly about in prodigious numbers. August is the main month for flying ants, which are a great factor in trout fishing, but September is the month for the largest of the ant family, the winged carpenter ants, and this is when they bring up the bass. Edward Hewitt claimed that ants have an acidic taste that is most attractive to fish.

At various times I have seen the surface of the Juniata River and Conodoguinet Creek peppered with amazing numbers of ants, and the fish were making the most of them. As Japanese-beetle fishing, one simply casts a light-weight surface lure to the rise rings, even though the mark on the water might seem insignificant.

The hellgrammite is an ugly-looking creature, and the fly it hatches into is not much better in appearance. The big long-winged Dobson fly moves about, mates, and deposits its eggs at night. If it were not for one aspect of its life cycle, it would not be the factor in bass fishing that it is. The eggs must be deposited on something that overhangs water. The egg masses appear as white splotches on the undersides of limbs and bridges. Upon emerging from the egg, the nymph drops into the water, to live there until it emerges as a fly, mates, and drops spent on the surface. The males may drop anywhere, but the females expire in the vicinity of the egg mass.

All this means that the holding water below bridges and overhanging limbs harbors bass that look for and take dying Dobson flies. Thus it is that the first good-looking water below a bridge is a prime spot for night fishing with a surface lure for feeding bass.

Most anglers will know of the seventeen-year locust. This cicada is appropriately named, for it is in the larval stage for more than sixteen years. It then emerges to procreate its kind. There are different broods for different areas, so that in one locale or another they are present every year. The Pennsylvania Department of Agriculture says there are nine broods in the state, one of which is of major significance.

Before 1936 I had never seen one, and that was to be the year for them at home. Advance notice warned that they would appear in plague proportions. The eggs would be deposited in the ends of branches, which would die and drop off so the newly hatched nymph could burrow into the earth. The number of dead locusts would be so great they would coat the ground. The incessant buzzing would make the air vibrate. They would be orange and black and slightly smaller than the common green locust.

At the time I did not know how they would fit into the

fishing picture, and I couldn't find anyone who knew from experience. Everything developed very much as prophesied, and I went fishing, first for trout and then for bass. The seventeen-year-old locust season turned out to be a hot-weather phenomenon—they appeared in July and August.

Many of the spent insects fell on the water, where they drifted in typical spent-wing fashion, buzzing spasmodically. The fact that the better trout took them suggested that interesting days were ahead with the bass, a more voracious species whose open season at that time corresponded more closely with the great locust emergence. In preparation and anticipation, I whittled small surface lures of an appropriate size and shape from blocks of red cedar.

Things worked well, then they worked exceedingly well. The bass ate the locusts as though life depended upon them alone. The smallmouths of our streams and the largemouths of our lakes became very surface-minded by day.

My homemade lures worked well, but they were a little light to cast well. This led me to try something different from anything I had attempted before. I tied on a Baby Popper, then added an imitation locust attached to an eight-inch dropper. Have you ever caught two bass on two different surface lures at the same time? Well, this combination did it, and it happened more than once in the seventeen-year-locust time. Oddly enough, these two lures did not travel straight ahead during the cast; they slowly rotated in flight, which was somewhat disconcerting. Since that year, we have had this cicada twice where I live, but I have intercepted various broods in other places. It can be expected to generate more action than usual, as well as more than usually interesting fishing.

Bass feed frequently on the surface, taking floating insects—both aquatic and terrestrial—very readily, and they have a greater tendency to forage for food than do trout, which usually take up a feeding position and let the current or the breeze deliver the food to them. Lest a false assumption be made, let me point out that there is a basic difference between the feeding activites of trout and bass. In our trout fishing we seek direct imitation as best we can, using a fly tied to suggest similarities with the natural, in the hope that the differences will be overlooked, and such flies are usually delivered to a trout that has taken a feeding position. This is what fly fisherman refer to as "matching the hatch." Close imitation is not a requirement with bass, because they are not selective to particular insects but will turn on anything that does not scare or startle them to the extent that they are made suspicious. The shape and color of a lure and the manner in which it performs matter little, though size is a factor. For surface-feeding insect-eating bass, my personal preference is for a ¼-ounce lure; nothing larger.

The big Conodoguinet Creek is the buggiest stream I've ever seen. The naturals there are not the common and popular trout-stream drakes but rather a group of warm-water hatches. Throughout August there is a big brown mayfly we call "the Chocolate Drake." The spinner (imago) of this insect leaves the foliage well before sundown to perform in its nuptial dance prior to depositing its eggs. For a period of one to two hours every evening for at least four weeks, unless there is rain or wind, the flies drop on the water and drift awash. Cruising bass are on the lookout for them and take them well. All the lure caster has to do is quickly cast to the observed location of such a feeder. The strike follows almost invariably.

Whereas drake fishing for bass is mostly on evening proposition, there are situations in which the presence of damsel flies is responsible for daytime surface activity on the part of both smallmouths and largemouths. This trim-bodied fly with biplane wings, whose color range goes from mustard brown to iridescent blue-black, has a distinctive trait—both males and females, or the two together, like to light and rest on the tips of weeds protruding above the surface. Bass like them so much that they jump out of the water in an attempt to pick them off the stems. In fact, they sometimes jump clear of the surface to intercept them in flight. The best way to find this kind of fishing is to go to areas that have considerable weed growth in August and September.

Weeded waters are no longer hard to find; today they are difficult to avoid. More and more chemical fertilizer is being used, and this has a greater tendency to wash off the ground than do the natural fertilizers. Considerable amounts of it accumulate in the silt beds of streams and lakes, producing a rich environment that is ideal for weed development. This is good up to a certain point; thereafter, it becomes a fisheries problem. In any case, it means that as time goes by there will be more and more damsel-fly fishing.

Grasshoppers, particularly those big ones with the yellow and yellow-green bodies, are the biggest, juiciest, and to the fish, the most appetizing insects of all. Bass love them. A hopper is different from most other insects that appear on the water in that it can propel itself on the surface. Other insects drift helplessly, but the hopper moves across the surface with strong kicks. They are poor fliers, and there is no reason to believe they can tell the difference between land and water. To make matters more interesting, the blue-ribbon environment for the big hopper is the high grass and cattails that abound along damp banks and shorelines. I have enjoyed fishing to hopper-eating bass where grazing cattle have sent them jumping into the water. There are times, too, when a wind will carry flying hoppers out over the water. Always there is that kicking, which is a real attention-getter. At hopper time I pay attention to the windward side of grassy banks. A small Spark Plug has become pretty much my standard lure for hopper fishing, but the Midge Oreno and Baby Popper are also satisfactory.

Casting to rising fish should be the rule in all types of water. Accuracy and distance casting are factors because the more skilled one is, the more fish can be shown the lure. The thoughtless are at a disadvantage when compared to the observant fellow who uses all information at his command.

After Dark

Under the cover of darkness most of the large bass wake up and, prodded by hunger, begin to move about. As the night shadows close in, the small bass taper off their feeding activity, and are ready for rest and sleep. A fish slumbers with its eyes open but things pass unnoticed, just as a mammal sleeps with its eardrums able to register sound waves, but does not comprehend normal sounds when asleep. By day we fish mainly for on-the-feed small bass and for a small minority of the big bass, whereas at night we fish for a majority of the bigger bass and very few small bass. Of course big and small are relative standards, and there are great variations between northern and southern bass and between smallmouths and largemouths.

Shallows offer a combination of food and cover, so that is where the forage fish will be found. At night the shallows become the feeding grounds of the predator. When on the feed, bass look for something moving, preferably something struggling or otherwise in trouble. The caster should pay particular attention to reeds, weeds, pads, cattails, rocks, and the shorelines, bays, and eddies. The change from day to night on a lake marks the changing of the guard for the bass, and I am sure for muskies too, though not for pike. Nature is not kind to her children. Everything in the wild hunts or is hunted, eats or is eaten, and the darkness is the time of the most dramatic stalks.

Lure-casting is a relatively young sport (fly fishing is many centuries older), but nevertheless it does have a considerable history. Let's crank back the time machine in the manner of H. G. Wells and go to the period between World War I and the Great Depression. This was the golden age of the economic boom, but what is probably more important to us now, it was also the golden age of the development of both lure-casting and fly-fishing.

The year was 1925. I was a teenager fishing with my Dad out of a nice lodge on Blue Sea Lake, Quebec. I will be forever grateful that Dad, who remained a duffer at fishing and hunting in spite of being an enthusiastic participant, always saw to it that I was well equipped. There were certain things he thought I should not have, but fishing tackle was not among those things. What I did with the equipment was up to me. Had he been able to advise and assist it would have been his joy; but the thing he could and did do was to encourage.

In the early years of my fishing education I was guided by two things, the first being my own observations and increasing experience, and the second being the fishing articles in outdoor magazines. Along with the big three of today—*Field and Stream, Outdoor Life,* and *Sports Afield*—there were at that time *Hunting and Fishing, National Sportsman,* and *Outdoor America.* My system was to check them at the stands, then buy the ones that contained articles that interested me.

One day I came across an article that disclosed the interesting information that bass could be caught at night, even on the darkest of nights, and that surface lures were best for such fishing. This, I am sure, was news to most of the lure fishermen of that time.

Dad was surprised but interested when he heard that I planned to fish Blue Sea at night for bass, for he knew I greatly preferred the group of small lakes of the area to big Blue Sea, and he had never heard of night casting.

Throughout the course of the week that had just passed, the smallmouths had been most uncooperative. The article had stated that when bass won't strike by day, they will by night, so there we were, crossing the broad bosom of the lake, headed for the uneven shoreline that was edged with reeds.

In the darkness of the night the water was smooth and unbroken. As we glided into casting position and the noises of the moving boat and the creaking oars became silent, only the calls of the night birds broke the silence. With our sense of sight restricted, the world around us shrank.

The lure that I had attached was the Pflueger Globe, because it was obvious from the description in the article that the Globe was the choice of the article's author. In those days there was a silly taboo against mentioning the names of commercial lures in articles, though such was not the case with flies, probably because names of fly patterns were usually not patented.

For half an hour nothing happened. I had settled down to methodical casting when a splash was heard back in the reeds. We eased the boat closer to the commotion. I made a cast in the direction of the sound. Night casting is different from the daytime operation because the lure cannot be seen in flight, and one can't always be sure exactly when it lands on the water. I had not yet reeled the slack out of my line when the stillness was broken by a great watery *glump.* This was more than the splashing of a feeding fish among the reeds. Something told me to haul back, and when I did, I was into a fish. In due course we boated a fine bass, and I had become an addict of night fishing for big bass, an addiction that has carried through the better part of a half century.

The contributor to that magazine was correct when he wrote that if you can't catch them by day, you can by night, and no doubt he started something with a considerable number of plug fishermen.

There are some things about night plugging that the novice ought to keep in mind. Here are a few such principles, in no particular order. It is not a good idea to use your lightest gear, for sooner or later you'll find yourself attached to a really powerful fish. A good boat, a lazy breeze, and a field of pads or a large submerged weedbed constitute an invitation to action. Currents in a stream and waves in a lake spoil the action of a top-water lure. The finest place in a river for night fishing is the fanned out area below a concentrated flow. The finest place in a stream is the tail of a flat. Night casting always provides a certain degree of solitude and primitive atmosphere, even when one is adjacent to the concrete jungle. The night fisherman should study the treeline and the landmarks by day, thereby establishing guidelines for after dark. It is important to strike by sound rather than by feeling, for many strikes cannot be felt, since bass do not always hit a slow-moving lure in a direction away from the fisherman.

The outdoor writers have often written that the darker the night, the better the fishing. I do not say they are wrong; they may be as right as rain; but my own preferences are otherwise. I love those eerie, soft moonlight nights when one can see where he is going and what he is doing. In the full of the moon it is possible to tie on a lure and unhook a bass without the aid of artificial light, and the jumps of fish can be seen. And to me, the moonlight night is more beautiful than the star-studded night, and both are more attractive than a black night. I operate on the theory that a night-feeder is a night-feeder whether the night is clear or cloudy, dull or dark.

One incident in particular remains vivid to me in spite of the fleeting years. Lambert Miller and I had chosen a shallow rock-strewn bay with a weed bed at each extremity as a likely feeding ground. We were on the water at night o'clock, though the full moon would not rise until midnight. For two hours in darkness we searched the pockets and submerged rocks with surface and underwater lures, but not a single strike was forthcoming.

The boat we had rented did not leak, so I spread out on the bottom, propped my head on a sweater, and fell asleep. Lambert may have been disgusted with the unsociability of his companion, but he was polite enough to be quiet. I must have slept for an hour or so before being suddenly awakened by a great splash. The moon was big and bright, and it appeared to be very close as it shone over the tops of the trees, illuminating the surface of the bay. I sat up drowsily and then realized that the splashing bass had Lambert's Plunker in its mouth. This was a call to arms.

My cast was promptly received by a fish. For at least an hour and a half we had the fastest action one could hope to experience. The place had come to life, and we were surrounded by willing strikes. Never before or since have I experienced such a great number of strikes at night, and they came from bass of all sizes. Before the moonlight touched the water we hooked nothing; after brightness engulfed the countryside, bass struck with reckless abandon, and one or the other or both of us were playing fish for the better part of two hours. By two a.m. we were satisfied to leave the charmed spot to get some rest for another day at work.

Many times bass lunge at surface baits without touching them, but once a large fish makes his noisy appearance, he can be marked down for future reference. The top-water lure is taken well at night, better than any other type of lure, and fortunately it is fairly snagproof and thus pleasant to fish. It is also an excellent fish-finder. Frequently bass are located at a certain spot and on an ensuing trip they are likely to be taken at exactly the same location and time of night. The limited areas where a fine fish is known to night feed in hot weather can be located by carefully observing and remembering the shape of the irregular skyline where the dark outline of the trees appears to touch the horizon.

One of my friends has become a night-casting specialist for big bass. Husky Frank Long is made of sturdy stuff, and he looks the part. By daytime he manages his store; by night he fishes. Normally he is an easygoing fellow, but during the bass season his life is vigorous and complicated. His enthusiasm and industriousness have occasionally held him on a stream all of a Saturday night, all day Sunday, and part of Sunday night. That is a lot of casting, and it involves a considerable loss of sleep, but he insists upon being, as much of the time as possible, at a place where big bass are located. When the weekend is over, he resumes his usual schedule of working by day, fishing by night, and sleeping—well, I just don't know where that fits into the picture.

Because of his concentration on night casting for stream or river smallmouth bass, Frank's conclusions and experiences are of particular interest. He tells me that in his first season of night fishing he caught forty-four bass over two pounds, six of which were over four pounds. His best night that year produced four bass that weighed a total of fourteen pounds. His largest fish that summer weighed five pounds, six ounces.

Frank's wide experience over a long period of time has led him to certain conclusions. His greatest success has been on moonlight nights, from mid-August to mid-September, during the hours of dusk to midnight. His favorite lures have been Jitterbug, Plunker, Crazy Crawler, and Crippled Minnow. He experienced more false strikes on the comparatively large Crippled Minnow, a propeller plug, than on any of the others. Lure color has made little or no difference. Most of the bass were taken from shallow water adjacent to deep pockets. More feeding fish that broke the surface took the lures than rejected them. Like all night-casters, he realizes the importance of striking by sound and striking at the least provocation. If nothing is hooked, he allows the lure to rest quietly for a few seconds, then he resumes the slow retrieve.

After plugging for several seasons, Frank decided to change his casting from the right hand to the left so that it would not be necessary to switch the rod from one hand to the other for the retrieve at the completion of each cast. After he mastered the left-hand cast, which was accomplished readily, he lost thirteen bass in succession before one was landed. He says, "With my left hand below the reel, I did not strike sharply enough at first to sink the hooks, and usually the bass got off on the first jump. I found it necessary to come up harder with the rod than I had previously done when I held it above the reel."

Frank was using bait-casting tackle, of course. With open-bail spinning gear, reeling is done with the left hand and striking with the right. But no matter what the equipment, strike back with authority. The larger the bass, the tougher its jaws. In order to sink a hook over the barb, it is necessary to move the lure in the mouth of the fish. A bass's mouth is tough, and there is stretch in the line when the strike comes at the end of a long cast. To offset such drawbacks, it is advisable to strike sharply and do so more than once with whatever tackle is employed, even when the lure is equipped with small, sharp, fine-wire hooks.

At the end of every fishing session I dry the line by casting in a low trajectory, then with fast reeling and a high rod tip rapidly recover the lure so that little or no line touches the water. With each cast some water flies from the line and reel until both are dry. It's interesting that on some nights this fast-skimming lure looks good to the bass. This could be called dry-line fishing.

There are fish that snap at and chase the lure without touching it. At times all the fish are inclined to do this. The big payoff is when strikes are coming so fast that it's difficult for the angler to call it a night.

In our region, the lure that became the local favorite for night fishing, and one that enjoys a great reputation among bass fishermen everywhere, is the black Jitterbug. During World War II the Arbogast Company substituted a selection of beautifully colored plastic mouthpieces for the original aluminum-alloy faces. This appeared to be a refinement, but things did not work out that way. The lightweight plastic face made the lure skip and bob more and gurgle less. The metal held the head in a slightly lower position, causing it to bore in and catch water, and that is what produces the famous Jitterbug commotion and sound.

Although I carry a special assortment of lures for my night bass fishing and switch about to some extent, as a result of trial and error, one lure has emerged the favorite. It is the Baby Popper with a rubber skirt glued around the midsection upside-down, so that when the plug is at rest in its normal vertical position, the skirt bows out and the individual "legs" work in the water. During the cast the legs fold back, offering little additional air resistance.

It can be said of night fishing that strikes from big bass can be confidently anticipated and that the man who fishes muskie water stands a good chance at encountering one of them. It is quite an experience to hook a big bass or muskie in the dark. Something else can be anticipated, and that is a quick response from the fish that one can hear feeding. Furthermore, there is a solitude to night fishing such as the daytime fishermen do not experience around centers of population.

New Frontiers

Two fairly recent developments have extended the angling frontier. The first of these two factors is the creation of impoundments; the second is an elaborate program of successful muskie propagation and distribution.

For the better part of the last decade my work has been in the field of land acquisition for the Pennsylvania Department of Forests and Waters. It has been the concept of the head of the Department, Dr. Maurice K. Goddard, an eminent ecologist, to have a green-park area featuring water-oriented recreation within a radius of twenty-five miles of every state resident; and it has been the concept of the Fish Commission to introduce bass, bluegill, sunfish, and muskies into new impoundments. Similar projects are taking place all around the land.

It is my conviction that a new, multipurpose artificial lake is a tremendous contribution if, and only if, a fine trout stream is not wiped out by the inundation. Man can create lakes, but he cannot create trout streams. However, by the use of deep-taps and low-flow augmentation he can create ribbons of cool trout water below large impoundments.

To a fisherman, the shoreline is the making of a lake. The more irregular it is, the better. To me, a small lake is more satisfactory to fish than a large lake. In a large lake one works up or down a shoreline; in a small lake one does the same, but there it is practical to shift back and forth from one side to the other.

My idea of a wonderful artificial fishing lake has several features. I would like it to be from fifty to five hundred acres in size, with a dam of not more than fifty feet in height. It should have bays and points and a shoreline studded with target and hazard spots. It would be best if it were to have a substantial source of cold water, so that fishing would hold up in hot weather.

I know that some engineers and biologists will scoff, but I do not quote it from the book, I tell it as I have seen it. Granted, fish do well in surface-drainage lakes, and such lakes have the advantage of not silting as much as the stream-fed bodies of water, but they have a horrible failing in that the hot-weather fishing in them ranges from poor to terrible. And take away July, August, and September and you have cut the heart out of the bass and muskie fishing time for most fishermen.

When man harms a body of water, it has ways of fighting back. For example, when chemical fertilizer is spread on the fields in the watershed above an impoundment, it has a tendency to wash off after rains, whereas manure goes into the earth. The fertilizer is carried into the impoundment, where it lodges in the bottom silt, thereby causing over-fertilization. Abnormal weed growth is the result. Some weed is a great thing, but too much is too much. Man can only retaliate with chemical treatment, but that is expensive, and the different varieties of weeds require different chemical treatments at different times.

My associate Bill Harmon, who has to contend with the weeds in Forest and Waters Department lakes in Pennsylvania, told me it cost the Commonwealth $6000 to successfully fight the weeds in 1240-acre Gifford Pinchot Lake for one year. It has been observed that aquatic growth is nonexistent or slight in water over twelve feet in depth, so the weed fighters like high dams in steep-sided valleys, because the impoundment so created will have little water that is less than twelve feet in depth. But it is the shallow water that furnishes the real fishing.

Newly inundated earth is rich—so rich, in fact, that it sustains a growth that is unparalleled by natural lakes and old impoundments. The nitrogen in newly flooded soil induces a tremendous growth of the floating microscopic organisms known as zooplankton. The abundance of such plankton as water fleas is reflected in the growth and condition of the fish.

I was the contact man in the acquisition of some rich agricultural land in York County, Pennsylvania. The little South Branch of the Codorus was dammed. The tap was closed and the storage started just at the time when an excess of muskie and northern pike fry had to be removed from the hatcheries. Early that summer some of each were planted in the pool of the dam, which was slowly increasing in size as it covered more and more earth. Few if any minnows were present. The available food was zooplankton. Three summers later the 3000-acre lake abounded with a visible supply of young game fish and hoards of bluegills. As green as it was, it was then opened to public fishing. To the surprise of all, pike over the twenty-four-inch legal limit were taken, as were largemouth bass up to sixteen inches. The muskies did not show up, probably because the northern pike got the jump on them in size and promptly gobbled them up. This great and rapid growth of both game fish and food fish had been sparked by a superabundance of plankton.

During the 60s most of the states and some of the federal agencies brought about the construction of many impoundments that are well located and much smaller than the power-generating giants of the Corps of Army Engineers. In many instances, the prime purpose of these impoundments was recreational opportunities, not the least of which is the combination of bass and muskie fishing. Some are, or will be, reservoirs for human consumption, others are part of flood-control projects, but the recreational aspect is considered equal in importance to the other factors.

Webster defines ecology as "biology dealing with mutual relations between organisms and their environment." Instead of ignoring the ecological relationships, it is time to examine them.

Procreation has always been the primary purpose of life; survival is the foremost desire of all creatures. The pressure of the balance of nature is felt by all. Each organism must submit to its separate purpose in its own complex environment. Every creature exists to eat or be eaten. The natural end is death, and nature is an impartial apportioner of that, yet the individual, through ingenuity, speed, strength, or subterfuge, may influence the time it occurs.

The naturalist Franklin Russell, in his masterful work *Searches at the Gulf*, puts it this way.

"Generation upon generation followed a pattern which over a long period stabilized things to such a high degree that their conduct was perfected. . . . The first-year creatures knew their time and place with utter precision, they knew exactly where they must go, though they had never been there; they knew exactly what they must do, though they had never done it before."

Nature is unconquerable. Man cannot win in a struggle against her, but he can live in harmony with her. She does not operate in separate compartments or with some circuits closed. Everything is interrelated and interdependent. Man calls this "the balance of nature."

Consider how the food chain operates in a stream or a lake. Algae, utilizing the inorganic substances, and bacteria, breaking down the organic matter, serve to make food available to all higher forms of life. These in turn serve as food for the microscopic zooplankton, the tiny "water fleas" that accelerate the entire food chain, thus increasing the water's carrying capacity and the rate of growth of larger forms of organic life.

The food webs are complicated. Aquatic life rarely exists on a straight food-chain basis. If it did, mild pollution would knock out everything. Aquatic life depends upon a variety of feeding relationships.

Nature's sanitary corps takes care of normal pollution, such as decaying leaves and remains of fish and animal droppings, but nature is not geared to cope with the unnatural pollutants. In healthy water there is a diversity of plant and animal species. Thus, contamination can be recognized by the lack of variety of living organisms.

Our second consideration in this story of the new frontier for the lure-caster has to do with muskies. In recent years we have seen improved muskie fishing in the old range and additional muskie fishing where not long ago there was no water and in other watersheds where not long ago there were no muskies. The muskie story is a success story of tremendous significance to those who like to cast a lure to game fish.

Compared with trout-propagation programs, a workable muskie program was slow in coming. First of all, an old concept had to be exploded, i.e., the false idea that big water of 300 acres and up was a requirement of the muskie.

The late Robert Page Lincoln fostered the theory that the lakes in Minnesota which had a natural population of muskies also harbored a certain red plankton and the waters which did not have the red plankton did not have muskies and that therefore the initial step in muskie distribution should be the introduction of the red plankton. My friend Bob has passed on, and I never heard more about his idea. It is my belief that, with a few exceptions, muskies now exist wherever fingerlings have been planted. The only doubtful question is whether there is a rate of natural reproduction in such waters.

A muskie does not build a nest. A pair simply swim about in shallow water, probably always close to the shoreline, and whenever the female drops eggs the male covers the area with a veil of milt. It is reputed that the life of the sperm is about forty-five seconds. If this living and life-giving organism does not quickly find and enter an egg, it dies.

Silt and algae-covered weeds kill fish eggs. Bass and sunfish clear the silt away from the nests they prepare, and after the eggs are deposited, the male guards the nest and periodically fans silt from it, thus accomplishing a good job of house cleaning. Muskies, on the other hand, drop their eggs and let them fall where they will. Those that land on silt and algae will rot before they can hatch, but some of those that land on gravel, stones, ledges, and sand may hatch. This being the case, the rate of natural reproduction in some bodies of water must be zero, and in many others the survival rate must be so low that the native population is hardly a factor. Under present fishing pressure, the hatch in even the best of waters is not great enough to support unrestricted killing. In the face of increasing pressure, the picture would appear to be a dark one, but there is more to the story, and all the rest is bright.

Before getting into the matters of introduction, redistribution, and supplementation of muskie populations, an examination of the natural range is in order. In a general way, the muskie is native to the northern part of the Mississippi River watershed. Included are three of the Great Lakes and the waters that drain into and from them. Lake Superior, essentially a trout lake, is too cold. There are feeders of the Mississippi that harbor muskies in no less than eight states. In addition to the upper Mississippi flowage, there is a native population in the watershed of the Saint Lawrence River.

The renowned muskie state is Wisconsin, even though only two watersheds in the north of the state are a part of the original range. Fortunately, they are large and beautiful systems featuring passage connections through numerous lakes. Involved are two beautiful rustic areas, the Manitowish and the Chippewa, each containing a substantial chain of lakes. This is the traditional muskie land. It was here that the muskie established its reputation. These waters were the testing places for many lures and the fishing grounds of many great anglers and celebrated guides. Hayward, Wisconsin, claims to be the Muskie Capital of the World.

Minnesota has its wonderful Mississippi River fisheries, which include lakes connected to the river. Saint Cloud is a central location. In addition there is the Mantrap Chain in the vicinity of Park Rapids.

Michigan has Lake Saint Clair. This lake produced a world-record fish, though the record was later broken by a Saint Lawrence River muskie. In addition there are some big inland lakes. Ironically, the great Saint Clair is so badly contaminated by Detroit that as of 1971 its fish may not be eaten.

Kentucky, Tennessee, West Virginia, and North Carolina have native muskie populations as well as muskie programs to supplement the existing supply and to increase the range.

Virginia and North Dakota have muskie-introduction programs.

North of the border the great muskie province of Canada is Ontario. In the west is the Lake of the Woods region and the Rainy River drainage. Further east is the Kwartha-Lakes–Trent-Canal section. The stocking program is most elaborate, and as in some of the states, an honest effort is being made to increase the range. This extension idea has already turned the Elephant and Baptiste Lakes systems into worthy muskie-fishing grounds.

The importance of these programs is emphasized when it is understood that following World War I fishing pressure intensified as pollution increased, with the result that muskie pop-

New York is blessed with two famous muskie fisheries, Chautauqua Lake and the Saint Lawrence River in the Thousand Islands area. Muskies have been successfully stocked in the Niagara River and Findley and Waneta lakes, among other New York waters.

Pennsylvania's native range is in the northwest part of the state. This encompasses the Allegheny River watershed, which includes Conneaut and LeBoeuf lakes, the Canamough River, and French Creek. The redistribution program has introduced muskies into the Susquehanna and its big feeder, the Juniata River, where they are doing extremely well. Some have been planted in the Delaware River and its big feeder, Perkiomen Creek. In addition they have gotten off to a great start in numerous impoundments in all portions of the state, both in acid and alkaline environments.

Ohio has a program that has made interest soar. The "beautiful" Ohio River, a part of the native range, is violently polluted, but there are still muskies in the feeder streams. Successful plantings have been made in various lakes and also in certain strip-mine waterways where the water is not too acidic.

ulations were dwindling and possibly disappearing. The first step was to hold the line on the take-home part of the reward. From a policy of just about anything goes, Ontario limited catches to two fish a day and set a thirty-inch-minimum size limit while at the same time tightening up on the number of fish that could be transported from the province. One by one, the muskie states followed suit. As this holding action prevailed, something was stirring behind the scenes.

In the great traditional muskie country biologists were conducting pertinent experiments. Wisconsin hatcherymen learned that ripe muskies could be trapped and tripped of eggs or milt. This had been a common practice with trout for a full century, though it does not work with bass and sunfish. It was then determined how the eggs could be held in batteries of jars with circulating water until they could hatch.

The next step was to learn how to provide the proper food for the young muskies, which when not properly fed turn on each other. The answer turned out to be a water flea known as *Daphnia*, and just the small ones at that. In their next stage of growth the hungry, fast-growing little predators had to be served tiny fish, though not necessarily members of the minnow family. Coordination was called for. Trial and error provided the answers. The eggs of various species of fish could be taken and hatched at the proper time for the express purpose of being converted into muskie flesh. First it was young fathead minnows, then golden shiners, and later suckers, carp, and trout. At Pennsylvania's great Linesville hatchery it was found that 10,000 fingerling muskies required 100,000 fry a day, sucker and carp by the millions being the groceries for this stage of muskie development. Then more mature golden shiners and fathead or spottail minnows are fed to the fingerlings until stocking time. Even with good feeding, some cannibalism takes place.

In the old days the term fingerling as applied to trout was taken literally and meant a fish of several inches. The muskie people applied a different and broader meaning having to do more with age than length. To them anything up to fourteen inches is a fingerling. This, I suppose, is their way of saying, "There is a tremendous difference between a four- and a four-teen-inch trout, but in our field a four- and a fourteen-inch muskie are much the same, both babies."

There followed a period of refinement involving many brains and many hands, and much observation, loving care, and trial and error. As the trappers and strippers designed new equipment and improved their techniques, the hatch-house department provided better egg-hatching facilities and feeders learned how to obtain fodder for their charges, both from the natural state and from egg-hatching batteries. Suckers, carp, trout, shiners, in fact almost anything but the basses could be provided and thereby become grist for the muskie mill. It appears that Hayward, Wisconsin, was the nerve center of this activity.

In New York State a decision was made to build a muskie hatchery at Chautauqua Lake in the hope of perpetuating that popular fishery. This project was different from many others in that trolling fishermen bought, built, and occupied the head-quarters, which included a cottage, a wharf, and a boat, along with muskie-fishing paraphernalia. Those who had to provide the future tackle-testers with food managed a few lakes so that their sole purpose was to raise little fish to be netted and deliv-ered to the Chautauqua Hatchery.

New York discovered, or more precisely rediscovered, that the stocking of fry did not pay off, but a suitable percentage of stocked fingerlings ultimately became legal game, and they pros-pered just as well, fought just as hard, and acted just the same as the natives of the lake. It was important that before being re-leased they be grown to a size that was too big for the bluegills and the rock bass to be able to handle.

In a well-conducted experiment in Green Lake, Wisconsin, it was determined that forty-five percent of the stocked muskie fingerlings survived to ultimately become legal-size fish.

In the years after World War II it became evident that the relatively new commercial fertilizers were contaminating the silt in the lakes and streambeds. They had become so rich that excessive weed growth had become a problem. This in turn produced bumper crops of bluegills in the lakes and rock bass in

Caught in Conneaut Lake in 1924, this 54 lb. 3 oz., 59 in. muskie remained the Pennsylvania record fish until 1972. Photo courtesy of Pennsylvania Fish Commission.

the streams. The result was a massive stunted population of bluegills and rock bass, which overwhelmed the baby bass. When it was time for the protecting male bass to leave the nest and forage for his food, the bluegills and the rock bass ate too many baby bass. What was needed was a predator that would feed heavily, summer and winter, on the excess bluegills and rock bass, thereby exerting a balancing effect. This is where the muskie entered the picture. It may sound like a paradox, but in our day a good predator is essential to good bass fishing.

A new day has dawned, a day when there are more muskies to fish for than there ever were before and when there are more waters in which to fish for them than there ever were before. And the best is yet to come.

Combination Fishing for Bass and Muskies

There is added excitement and appeal when one fishes for bass and muskies at the same time. These two great fresh-water game fish are similar enough in their striking proclivities to make it practical to fish for both at once, yet they are different enough to bring into play conflicting approaches. In order to do justice to both, one must make certain concessions involving a readjustment of tackle in general and lures in particular. This, I believe, has greater appeal to the average angler than the approach of the specialist who concentrates on one at the expense of the other.

Throughout all of our fishing we give a little here to gain a little there, and this is especially the case with what might be called "combination fishing" for bass and muskies.

Stream smallmouths, which are usually found in relatively shallow water, respond best to lures in the ¼-ounce class. The spat of a light lure on the water attracts them, whereas the heavy-hitting splash of a larger lure startles them and puts them down. And the light lure matches the size of the foods they most commonly consume, middle-size crayfish in particular.

Bigmouths of the lakes are normally located in deeper water and are therefore less likely to be alarmed by the lure hitting the surface. Furthermore, true to their name, their mouths are bigger, therefore it is reasonable to assume they are capable of handling larger mouthfuls than their less ubiquitous cousins. A ⅜-ounce lure is usually ideal for lake fishing for largemouth bass.

Muskies, on the other hand, are generally fished for with a five-inch, ¾-ounce lure, and even larger ones are sometimes used. This is because they are primarily small-fish eaters. One look at a muskie's mouth is enough to make this evident.

When we turn to casting equipment, about the same principles apply. Go light for smallmouths, heavier for bigmouths, and heaviest for muskies. There are reasons why muskies call for fairly heavy tackle. First, the added strength is needed to boss a hooked muskie; second, the added heft is needed to cast a heavier lure.

If we increase slightly both the size of the ideal bass lure and the strength and backbone of the ideal casting equipment, while decreasing both the size of the muskie lure and the strength of the equipment, we are still in the ball park for both bass and muskies. This happy compromise permits one to think bass and muskies at the same time. In all our fresh-water angling, this, to me, is the classic example of compensating factors at work.

Having taken the realistic approach of going a little heavier for bass and a little lighter for muskies, we can now make a selection of a specific lure. My choice is a skim and swim lure, specifically the ½-ounce Whirligig, a metal-and-wood combination.

Because the Whirligig is so intricate that it may never be placed on the market, an explanation of how to construct it is incorporated in the lure-making chapter, so that a person can either make his own or turn to some handyman for help.

My favorite muskie color is metallic green, with hot copper as a close second, and I like yellow and frog finish best for bass. It is a simple matter to paint Whirligig in any of these finishes or in any combination of them. One paint job I depend upon is green with a yellow head, another is copper with a green head, and a third is the old reliable yellow with a red head.

Combination Fishing for Bass and Muskies

The only plug ever designed that casts better on balanced tackle than Whirligig is the dummy plug used for tournament casting. The Whirligig is a great one for reaching far and wide and for the best possible accuracy.

A common practice is to permit a floater to land and lie idle as the rings on the surface widen, and then to activate it with rod-tip action, followed by another rest—then the stop-and-start retrieve. Time has demonstrated that this is effective on bass, but maybe there is a better retrieve for combination fishing.

If the delivery is a flat cast, that is, one of low trajectory, and the rod tip is hauled back as the lure touches the surface, the result is a flat, skidding entry in the direction of the caster. This is both lifelike and attention-getting. Bass respond to it well, and muskies, and pike too, greatly prefer it to the dead-lure landing. This is easily accomplished with the multiplying reel on either the conventional bait-casting rod or the new-style spin-casting straight-handle rod, but the skilled spinning fisherman with the open-face reel and the accomplished spin-caster with the push-button reel can manage this entry too.

The surface action of Whirligig is unique and something to behold. It bobs and weaves and turns from side to side as the twirling head splatters a fine watery spray. It lends itself to artistic toying, and the caster of lures for muskies is by necessity an artist. It would appear from the construction of this lure that the underwater action would be straight ahead without wabble, like a sinking propeller plug, but such is not the case. The metal ears, which also make the head rotate, draw the lure from side to side in a most enticing wabble.

From the cast, to the surface play, to the swim back, this is an amazing lure. Even in the old days of craftsmanship and handwork there was nothing that fished like it, and in this age of volume production, short-cuts, and simplicity a commerical lure probably cannot be manufactured to do what it does in its capacity as a lure for combination fishing—muskies and bass, surface and underwater.

One year scuttlebutt along the Conodoguinet Creek had to do with something new and different. The previous October two muskies were said to have been caught in the flat above Weighs

Bridge, and after that another was lost. Still another report was that golfers at the fourteenth hole were seeing a muskie downstream from Samples Bridge. A third story centered around "giant pickerel" seen by boys in a big downstream flat, though no pickerel were ever reported having been taken locally from a limestone stream such as this, it being thought that these streams are too alkaline to suit chain pickerel.

Up till that time no fingerling muskies had been stocked in the Conodoguinet Creek, although fish could enter it from the Susquehanna River, and conceivably they might spill over the dam that forms sixty-acre 'Possum Lake and follow the little outlet stream to the big creek. In any case, reports indicated that muskies were becoming a part of the Conodoguinet fauna. This was an exciting prospect to me.

In anticipation of bass-muskie combination fishing I had made up a batch of ½-ounce Whirligigs. The first one to hit the water was an all-yellow job, and the place was the Weighs Bridge flat. I arrived and started casting well before dark, intending to loiter around for an hour or two that evening. It was the time of the year when the chill of night had cooled the water.

The last time I had fished that spot there was a little bar across the way, the kind where one drinks, not wades. It was on the high-bank side of the stream. It had since been remodeled into a handsome tavern. About the time the horizon took on a velvety appearance somebody inside the tavern threw a switch and an array of large, soft, variously colored lights lit up the building and the streamside parking lot. I faced the lights from the far side of the stream, and the reflections in the water appeared even brighter than the lights on the posts. Never before had I thought that I would like to see a good fishery lose its isolated character before the invasion of civilization, but suddenly I found myself angling in a fairyland with its own peculiar domesticated beauty.

First I put Whirligig into a long green reflection. I could see the splash, and then behind the bobbing and weaving plug an undulating V disrupted the greenly glowing surface. Then I went for the yellow beam. Then the blue. It was like a game. As the lure belly danced toward me down the eerie blue reflection, I asked myself a pertinent question: Is it the lure or the way it is worked that does the job? Or do we depend on fish temperament? The answers to these questions may be beyond the knowledge of man, but my vote goes to the first two factors in combination.

Suddenly there was an abrupt commotion as the symmetry of the blue strip was shattered and a watery thrust disrupted the surface and a splash broke the stillness of the night. For a split second I saw the blue light shining on a very long back. I felt nothing, and I did not hook the fish, nor did anything happen thereafter.

I left the creek that night having experienced no engagement with a great battler, but I had no doubt that the neon-lighted water held the potential for such an experience. The Weighs Bridge flat harbored a muskie as long as your leg.

The next visit to this artificial fairyland produced results, though not of the sort I had expected. It was a bass, and a big one, that rent the silence and distorted the reflections, but this time a hook sank home and everything held. Three times that bass jumped and many times he surged and rolled, distorting and mixing the colors of the illuminated surface.

This turned out to be my best smallmouth of the season, and it came while I was deeply involved in combination bass and muskie fishing. I don't know if he rose to the surface-darting action because of hunger, ire, or love of the chase, but rise he did and only he knew why. This was a wonderful interlude in my continuing campaign for that big muskie, which as of this writing, I'm sure is still there.

I love the Conodoguinet. An exaggerated story that is told of the long stream illustrates a significant point. Two canoeists were paddling their way upstream. One evening when it was time to set up camp they came to a beautiful meadow with a farm and barn up on the flat above the hill. They went up to the farmhouse for permission to build a campfire by the stream, and while there they bought some butter, eggs, and milk.

Early the next morning they broke camp and paddled up the stream all day long. As evening was approaching, they came to

A few remarks about the differing habits of bass and muskies may be in order. There is no such thing as muskie-infested water, but concentrations of bass are normal. A muskie will pre-empt a location and jealously guard the area. Bass enjoy the company of kith and kin and move about socially together. A muskie usually hits with the throttle wide open, showing an unsurpassed viciousness. A bass may do anything. Courage and zeal mark a bass that is defending its nest, whereas a muskie defends neither eggs nor young; in fact, muskies do not make nests. A muskie seems to deliberate more about striking, often times following a lure, whereas the reactions of bass are usually spontaneous. Of the two, the muskie is certainly more mysterious, unpredictable, and temperamental.

One day, in answer to my fondness for wading and casting, I took the combination bass-muskie lure to the Susquehanna in the expectation of catching some bass and in the hope of hooking a muskie. A sort of bay formed by large submerged rocks was my target for the evening. I supposed that the rocks had been left there by a melting glacier as it retreated northward.

The bass took the lure with satisfying regularity, but the muskies wouldn't cooperate. Suddenly a muskie rolled up, facing my way, right where I had been working the plug on the surface. When I told a muskie-fishing friend about this, his reaction was, "He knew something out of the ordinary was going on, and he wanted to have a look above the waterline to a suitable place to pitch camp. On the hill above was a farmhouse and barn. When they walked up to the farm to ask permission to camp and to replenish their diminishing larder, they were greeted by a familiar figure who said, "Hello, so you are back again." Then she pointed down the bank on the opposite side of the house and remarked, "Down there is where you spent last night."

The loops in the Conodoguinet are wonderful. There are two in particular that I periodically fish. You can park the car, walk a hundred yards in one direction, fish the mile or so of stream bend, and end up a hundred yards in the other direction from the car.

Combination Fishing for Bass and Muskies

see what it was." I think he was right, for since then I've seen this same thing happen a good number of times.

The story told by R. R. Souder Sr. of Williamsport, Pennsylvania will illustrate the muskies' proclivity for cussidness.

"Time was running out for an angler who wanted desperately to catch his first 'lunge. He was told that as a last resort hook up a live rat and permit it to swim over the known location of a big muskie. With great complication and cost he managed to obtain six live-trapped rats. The guide hooked up one by the scuff of the neck and it was placed overboard to swim. In due time the rat, untouched by a muskie, drowned and was rendered useless. The same thing happened to the other rats until the fisherman was down to his last one. Before the guide could hook up rat number six, it bit him, jumped overboard and swam away from the boat. That rat the muskie took."

The fact that it is practical to fish for bass and muskies, or bass and northern pike, for that matter, at the same time is sure to become well known. This sort of fishing has an appeal that will grow with the increasing muskie range, as new impoundments are created and muskies are introduced into these and into existing waters.

What motivates a bass does not necessarily trigger off a muskie or pike. There are few points in combination muskie and bass fishing where it can be said that this is right and that is wrong. By and large, I think the greatest difference between them is in their preferences in speed of retrieve. Muskies like it fast, bass like it deliberate. The angler, of course, is in charge, for he regulates the pace of the retrieve to suit his fancy under different circumstances. It does not appear to be motion alone or a given lure alone that attracts, but rather a combination of the two. My experience and observation indicate that the skim-and-swim technique with the Whirligig is a realistic answer to the problem of how to simultaneously combine bass and muskie fishing.

The picture of a new world-record breaker, a 67 lb. 8 oz. muskie caught by Cal Johnson, an outdoor writer, was widely published and possibly seen by more people than any other photograph of a fish, for Cal furnished all fellow outdoor writers with a printer's mat. Photo courtesy of Wisconsin Natural Resources Dept.

Muskie and Bass Reports

It is obvious that in the face of increasing pressures the muskie would be in deep trouble without the assistance of man. It is obvious, too, that the only way in which muskies can be introduced into new, isolated waters is by the hand of man. It is also obvious that there are many new impoundments where muskies could be given a chance by introductory or periodic stockings. Add to these facts the need for a good predator to help hold the line on vast populations of bluegills in the lakes and rock bass in the streams—which by their very numbers overpower the baby bass directly after the protective custody of the male terminates—and you have four good reasons for stocking muskellunge.

A good fisheries program sells itself. Thanks to good management, the muskie situation is not deteriorating but improving, and as muskies increase, the bass situation also improves.

The following reports are examples of what is transpiring in Chautauqua Lake, New York. Both were published in the excellent *Bulletin* of the Sport Fishing Institute, Washington, D.C.

1968

"During the 1968 season Chautauqua Lake muskalonge anglers experienced the best fishing since 1962. The catch was nearly 7,000 legal-size fish, averaging 33.3 inches long and 9.5 pounds in weight. The final tabulation of data supplied by cooperative anglers who fished the 13,000-acre lake, as reported by Stephen R. Mooradian, fishery biologist in Olean, New York, indicated a yield of 5.5 pounds of musky per surface acre. That is an average yield of one legal size musky for each 1.72 acres.

"Approximately 17,000 anglers purchased the special muskalonge license in 1968, with 23 per cent of the total successfully landing one or more legal muskies. This success ratio was found to be the best in the past ten years. Successful anglers fished an average of 43 hours for each muskalonge harvested.

"Anglers traveled from 23 states and Canada to fish the famed Chautauqua Lake in 1968. New York state residents accounted for 68 per cent of the total anglers, with 16 per cent from Pennsylvania, and 13 per cent from Ohio.

"The 1968 musky harvest from the other stocked waters in Cattaraugus and Chautauqua counties of New York was: Cassadaga Lake—240 fish; Conewango Creek—127 fish; Bear Lake—68 fish; Findley Lake—59 fish; and Allegheny River—Olean Creek—136 fish.

1971

"A recent report from fishery biologist Stephen R. Mooradian, Department of Environmental Conservation, Olean, New York, indicated that a total of 5,856 muskellunge ("muskalonge," in New York) 30 inches long and larger were harvested in 1971 from waters in Cattaraugus and Chautauqua counties. Chautauqua Lake, alone, supplied over 90 per cent (5,304) of these prize game fish. Their average length was 34 inches and their average weight was 10.3 pounds. This is equivalent, in terms of production, to 4.2 pounds of musky per surface area. In other words, it required the productivity of nearly 2½ acres to provide one legal-sized muskellunge to the angler-catch.

"One-fifth of the 15,320 licensed muskellunge fishermen were successful in landing one or more legal fish. The successful anglers averaged 33 hours to land each legal muskellunge. The best month to harvest musky was July, with 25% of the catch, followed by August with 23%, September with 20%, October with 10%, and June with 14%. The best months for catching large muskellunge (40 inches or over) were June and October. Anglers from 26 states fished Chautauqua Lake during the 1971 season. New York residents comprised 70.5 per cent, with Ohio contributing 14.1 per cent and Pennsylvania 12.4 per cent. The remaining states contributed between one and thirty anglers each."

The Pennsylvania Fish Commission publishes an annual muskie report in bulletin form of large format that spells out the places and numbers of the stockings of both fingerlings and fry. Except for the record of the individual stocking points, much of the text of the 1972 report is herewith printed with the permission of the Pennsylvania Fish Commission:

"A muskellunge program is not new in Pennsylvania. At least the propagation and stocking of fry dates to the nineteenth century. In 1894, fifteen large muskellunge were stocked and in 1896 and 1897, 91,000 fry were planted from the Western Hatchery (Corry Hatchery). In four different years from 1905 to 1917 muskellunge fry hatched from eggs received from New York State were planted in lakes in the western counties which already had an indigenous muskellunge population.

"One of the new features of the Fish Commission's program, started in 1953, is the introduction of muskellunge into lakes newly built by the Pennsylvania Fish Commission, Department of Forests and Waters, water supply reservoirs and existing waters not heretofore populated by this species. In other words, an attempt is being made to extend the range of the muskellunge. In the 'old days' the fry were planted in the natural range of the muskellunge which consisted of the upper Allegheny River Basin, the Lake Erie drainage and Lake Erie. In fact, these plantings may some day confuse fishery taxonomists (biologists who classify fishes according to their natural relationships). These taxonomists recognize at least three subspecies of muskellunge, one of which is the Ohio musky from Lake Chautauqua, and another is the Great Lakes muskellunge found in Lake Erie. Since the Pennsylvania muskellunge fry propagated in the Western Hatchery originating from eggs from the Lake Chautauqua muskellunge were planted in Lake Erie and Presque Isle Bay in 1912 and 1913, taxonomists will probably find the differentiation of these subspecies more and more difficult.

"To get back to our story, one of the problems encountered during the 1950's when the new program was struggling to get underway was the difficulty in hatching eggs and rearing fry and fingerlings in good numbers.

"Up until 1969-70 losses on eggs and fry amounted to almost 95 percent, and this occurred even when techniques effective in other states were adopted. These mortalities were not something recent. Even though many fry were planted in some years before World War I, in three of the seven years that over a half million eggs were received from New York, no fry survived to be planted in Pennsylvania. These early fish culturists had their problems but no research followed to alleviate this difficulty.

"It became obvious that at this time research was needed badly. In 1960, a cooperative research program was initiated with the propagation, law enforcement and research divisions all pitching in to start a crash program to improve the muskellunge fishing in the Commonwealth by improving techniques of production. By 1964, this effort had paid off in a big way. Egg hatching had been increased from 5 to 82 per cent and fry survival to fingerling sizes of 2 to 8 inches amounted to an amazing 90 per cent. Even in trout culture this would be an excellent survival rate. This research was culminated with a publication describing the new methods in a leading technical journal.

"The next step in the program was to determine whether muskellunge would survive and would grow in their new range. This is a difficult problem since, under natural conditions, only one out of every thousand fry survives to the fingerling stage where they can be seen and counted. Then, as in other stable communities of life, only two will live to replace their progenitors in the spawning population. This may be from 20,000 to 25,000 eggs originally produced by one female. All of this added up to one huge problem for the biologist.

"Indeed, planting of muskellunge fry and fingerlings under certain conditions did produce satisfying results. An early spring trapnet catch in 1966 on little 137-acre Hills Creek Dam in Tioga County, first stocked in 1958, produced five legal muskellunge in one night, one of which exceeded 42 inches. The Fish Commission's Somerset Lake in Somerset County yielded 18 legal muskellunge to the spring trapnets after the fish had been in there only six years. The greatest boon of all was the returns from muskellunge introduced in the Susquehanna River near Harrisburg in 1958. The so-called Falmouth muskellunge fishery has gained a national reputation for its excellence. During the early spring fishing almost 100 muskellunge are taken with many going over 40 inches. Eighteen have been reported captured in one week in this locality.

"It has been just in recent years that anglers have had an opportunity to angle for this prize game fish in all areas of the state. Previous to the 1950's the fry were planted only in the western lakes. At the turn of the century the 'powers that be' at that time felt that the muskellunge would eat all the other fish when introduced into a new lake. Why they felt they would eat all the fish in a new introduction and not in the lakes in which they already existed is something to contemplate upon. Be this as it may, one of the reasons for the new introductions in the modern program is to establish a large predator which will aid in controlling excessive fish populations. This, of course, is for the betterment of both pan fish and game fish.

"The muskellunge have some indirect benefits which many an angler is quick to admit, because even though he may not be fishing for this king-of-the-pikes, he is apt to hold his breath when he casts into a likely spot, sort of inwardly hoping and expecting a musky strike. So much has been written on individual experiences on catching muskies that it would be repetitious to list them here. However, we can add a few items that biologists have learned about the fish and fishing that may be of some aid to a musky fisherman.

"One of the first requirements of a muskellunge angler is perseverance. Creel censuses have shown that it takes between 75 hours and 150 hours to catch a muskellunge on good musky waters. This will vary with the fisherman and the season. Late spring and early fall fishing is considered the best because it has been found that muskellunge fast for a few weeks during the summer. Also the failure to catch muskellunge during the summer may be due to the abundance of available food, retirement to deep water and sluggishness induced by warm water. It is not due to the shedding of teeth, for these are shed constantly throughout the year.

"Why doesn't the Fish Commission rear as many muskies as they do trout? There are many reasons, but the limiting factor is food. Muskellunge will eat only live food and when they start eating small fish, their food consumption is enormous. At the Linesville Hatchery, 10,000 young fingerling muskellunge were eating an estimated 100,000 small minnows a day. Can you imagine the food consumption if 2,000,000 muskellunge were reared to yearling size!

"Creel limits and size limits are another method of aiding a muskellunge population, but most important in the management of any highly regarded sport fish are techniques to insure an annual recruitment of young fish. Good fishing results from a dependable annual replenishment.

"The first step in Pennsylvania's program is to introduce the muskellunge into as many suitable water areas as possible. If these introductions are successful and the muskies reproduce, some day Pennsylvania's extended muskellunge area may bring this fine game fish within reach of all the anglers in the Commonwealth and also help to produce better fishing for all species.

"This, in brief, is the new muskellunge program:

"1. To develop new and better methods for rearing more forage fish, so that muskellunge fingerlings of greater size can be stocked.

"2. To extend the range of the muskellunge so that fishermen have access to these fish.

"3. To use the muskellunge as a predator to help balance fish populations.

"4. To learn the habits of this fish, so that management techniques may be improved and fishermen may have a better chance of catching one.

"This is the program, and from the responses which came to this office, it looks as though the fishermen of the Commonwealth agree with this new project. The Commission's continuing research program on muskellunge culture is paying off annually in more fish stocked and more caught in more waters of the Commonwealth.

"In 1966, 351,500 fry and 69,481 fingerlings were stocked in streams, rivers, and lakes in 35 counties. The Commission is endeavoring each year to hold more fingerlings for fall planting, since the survival at this stage is greater than when planted earlier.

"In 1971, 971,000 fry and 51,400 fingerlings were planted at 80 stocking points in 43 of the 67 counties.

"The native home of the muskellunge in Pennsylvania is in the northwestern lakes, and it is here each spring that hatchery men and enforcement personnel live-trap breeders and collect spawn. Eggs are incubated at two northwest hatcheries: Union City and Linesville.

"The Commission's program for musky stocking now includes waters in all regions of the state. The lakes where breeders were taken are stocked annually, and the remaining are distributed in other lakes and rivers which have suitable musky habitat. As a result of the stocking program, muskellunge are now found in 50 waters where they did not occur naturally.

"It is gratifying to note that in practically all waters where muskies have been introduced catches of legal-size fish have been made after three years. Because of the growing enthusiasm among anglers for the musky, the Commission has formed a 'Husky-Musky Club,' which gives recognition to successful anglers for this giant of the game species. Records compiled by the Club will be a value in future muskellunge management."

"Persistence, more than any other characteristic a fisherman may possess, is the keynote to musky fishing success. In a recent report on the Ohio muskellunge program, 1948 to 1958, by Ray H. Riethmiller of the Ohio Division of Wildlife, it was stated that the average time devoted to account for one musky in Ohio was 100 hours of fishing, and this by 'specialists.' The rate decreased to one musky per one thousand hours of fishing for those of lesser talents. In other waters claims of one musky for every 8 to 10 hours of fishing have been made.

"Just how complete or accurate such figures are would be most difficult to substantiate, because musky fishermen, unlike their brothers concerned with the 'lesser' species, are not prone to brag. Many hide their enthusiasm and their successes, lest they get too much company."

Programs such as these, which are being conducted in various states and provinces, point out an amazing fact—the best muskie fishing is yet to come.

Bass Report

The following historical data relative to the distribution of bass has been taken from the chapter, "Bass and Bass Craft", of the book, *The Eastern Trail* written by members of the Pennsylvania Outdoor Writers Association.

Neither largemouth or smallmouth bass were native to New England, the waters west of the Rockies, or to the Middle Atlantic States east of the Allegheny Mountains. The redistribution of them was fantastic, much of the story being told years ago by Dr. Henshall. The introductory timetable was as follows:

Fox Lake, Massachusetts	1850
Many lakes in Connecticut	1852
Potomac River in Maryland	1854
New Hampshire	1867
Six lakes in Maine	1869
Thirty lakes in Rhode Island	1870
Susquehanna River in Pennsylvania	1873

It is interesting to note that Maine secured its bass from New York State. Pennsylvania was first stocked with Maryland bass. In these plantings differentiation was not usually made between smallmouths and largemouths.

Dr. Henshall's report of the initial Maryland stocking was well documented. John Eoff of Wheeling, West Virginia, entered the following into the 1854 report of the Smithsonian Institution: "Mr. William Shriver, a gentleman of this place, and son of the late David Shriver, Esquire, of Cumberland, Maryland, thinking the Potomac River admirably suited to the cultivation of the bass, has commenced the laudable undertaking of stocking that river with them; he has already taken, this last season, some twenty or more in a live-box, in the water tank on the locomotive, and placed them in the canal basin at Cumberland, where we are in hopes they will expand and do well, and be a nucleus from which the stock will soon spread.'' General Shriver, reports Dr. Henshall, in a letter to Philip T. Tyson, of Baltimore, Agricultural Chemist of Maryland, in September, 1860, says: ''The enterprise or experiment was contemplated by me long before the completion of the Baltimore and Ohio Railroad to the Ohio River at Wheeling, but no satisfactory mode of transportation presented itself to my mind until after the completion of the great work (in, I believe, the year 1853), and in the following year I made my first trip (although I made several afterwards in the same year), carrying with me my first lot of fish in a large tin bucket, perforated, and which I made to fit the opening in the water tank attached to the locomotive, which was supplied with fresh water at the regular water stations along the line of the road, and thereby succeeded well in keeping the fish (which were young and small, having been selected for the purpose) alive, fresh, and sound.

''This lot of fish, as well as every subsequent one, on my arrival at Cumberland were put into the basin of the Chesapeake and Ohio Canal, from which they had free egress and ingress to the Potomac River and its tributaries, both above and below the dam.''

General Shriver also states in a subsequent letter to Dr. Asa Wall, of Winchester, Virginia, dated September 17, 1867: ''The number of these black bass taken to the Potomac River by me, as well as I can now recollect, was about thirty.''

Henshall further advised: ''Private citizens of Pennsylvania introduced the black bass (smallmouth) into the Susquehanna about 1869, at Harrisburg. In 1873 the tributaries of the Susquehanna, the Potomac, and Delaware Rivers were supplied with black bass by the Commissioners at thirty-five different points.''

By the turn of the century there was a vast native population in many waters of various states. Everywhere it seemed to be the case of a little going a long long way. Early in the twentieth century the Pennsylvania fishermen called them, ''the new fish.''

Judging by recreational and economic values, the introduction of both largemouth and smallmouth bass into new waters is conservation's brightest success story, not only of that age but for all ages. When the angler counts his blessings, he can thank his lucky stars for the foresight, energy, and activity of some fishermen who preceded him.

The scale of a fish develops in circumference in the form of growth rings in proportion to body development. The greatest growth takes place when feeding activity is at its maximum, the least when feeding is at its minimum. This is controlled by body temperature, which in actuality is water temperature. When the scale is enlarged, these two annual seasons appear much as the growth rings on the sawed-off portion of a tree trunk.

A bass scale is translucent. When cemented to a piece of glass (with a clear substance) that will fit into an enlarger, then with the light blacked out all around the scale with paint, the scale becomes a negative from which a print can be made. This bass was in its sixth year.

Casting

The little group was so closely knit that it might have been called "the Possum Lake Casters' Association," but there was nothing official about it. An interesting code came into being in much the same manner as Topsy. It just grew. The standard operating procedure was for each to advise the other three of each newly discovered location of a muskie or a big bass. When one tested a new commerical lure that pleased him, or came up with some interesting homemade offering, he demonstrated it to the others. This collective information was of considerable value. So it was that dope on fish and lures was shared, but this was not the case with tackle.

Each went about his job in a different manner. Norm Lightner employed a Mitchell 300 open-face reel, a sturdy steel rod, and a fifteen-pound-test monofilament line. The John Rex reel was the large encased Zebco, which he used with a Heddon Brute Stick and an eighteen-pound-test monofilament line. Dan Gardside used an open-face reel, a fiber glass surf rod, and twenty-pound-test monofilament. I fish with a Shakespeare Hydro-Flo quadruple-multiplying reel, a six-foot straight-handle spin-casting rod, and twenty-five-pound-test Micron floating line with a five foot fifteen-pound-test monofilament casting trace. John and Don cast with two hands, Norm and I with one. Each was satisfied with his method of delivery, and certainly each did better with the tackle he favored than any one of the others could have done with it.

There is no need to employ a lure that does not cast well on your outfit. Any lure that lacks the necessary weight or offers excessive air resistance should be eliminated. Pulling-power and streamlining are important factors. It does not make sense to pitch something that starts out and rides like a potato chip.

Is it not accurate to say, "Casting takes a day to learn and a lifetime to perfect"? This brings up the matter of what constitutes good casting. The target must be regularly hit with uncanny accuracy. Extreme range for certain situations should be 125 feet and upwards. The trajectory should be low, so the proper entry of the lure can be effected. Why is trajectory important? Let's go back to the days and writings of Sheridan R. Jones, who was described in 1962 by Robert Page Lincoln as "the great fisherman who disappeared."

The second book that I added to what is now my quite respectable angling library was purchased in 1929, but the first edition came off the press in 1924. *Black Bass and Bass Craft* by Sheridan R. Jones took its place beside Dr. Alexander Henshall's *The Book of the Black Bass*. I read, reread, and poured over both books, as witness today their well-worn pages, when I should have been devoting time to mathematics, language, and economics assignments. Lafayette was good to me, but I did not do justice to that great little college.

This was a time when the large lure, delivered with that great American invention, the badly named bait-casting outfit, reigned supreme. Sheridan Jones fostered the ideas that, to be more effective on bass, lures should be reduced in size, and, in order to cast them better, the rod should be increased in length. He was a champion of the Al Foss pork-rind rigs because they were the smallest and most compact lures that were then available. It should be noted that much of his bass fishing was for stream smallmouths.

Jones had a third idea that went hand in hand with his diminution approach. It had to do with lure entry. He called his method "the silent dive cast," and a complete chapter of his bass book was devoted to it. I have never read another passage in the hope of improving my angling that has had as great an impact and has been of as much use as the following quotation, pages 160-168, from *Black Bass and Bass Craft*.

"Taking bass water as it comes and goes, bass weather day in and day out, bass temperament in spring, summer and fall, bass moods in sunshine and in cloud, in daylight and in dark, we believe that the silent cast will draw the more strikes, raise the larger fish, and receive a strike that will be the better hooked than will a cast that strikes the water with a splash and a commotion. The strike at a splash cast is frequently nothing but a butting rush—the lure may be knocked high into the air. We usually find that a bass hits a silently cast offering with his mouth wide open.

"Regardless of how ardently anglers recommend the overhead cast with the bait-casting tool, it is interesting to note how many expert bait-casters regularly use the 'side-swipe' or underhand cast when actually fishing. Now they all know that they are sacrificing accuracy; that such a cast is dangerous when fishing in company with other casters; that they cannot hope to get distance with this cast; and that the tournament boys are all making fun of their efforts—but they also know that they can place a lure with the lightness of a bit of cork with the underhand cast, something that is impossible with the standard overhead method. They also know that this method favors a prompt return of the lure—the start being made before the offering touches the water. We do not wish to give the impression that all silent casting is done *à la* the 'side-swipe.' Far from it, but this method is frequently employed when the overhead cast seems too strenuous as a commotion maker.

"While we are on this subject of the terminal end of the cast, it might be well to point out that a great many anglers fail in their casting at, what we believe to be, the critical point. Many are content to shoot out a nice line and to have the lure fall with reasonable accuracy at the desired spot. Here is where they fail. A lure, especially a plug, should never fall into the water—it should dive into it. Not only must the offering be checked over the desired area, but the return must be started as the plug drops toward the surface. In this way a bit of expert work will put a lure into the water with as pretty a dive as was ever executed by a professional swimmer. No splash about it—just a clean-cut dive.

"This is not only a fancy bit of tip work that looks pretty from the point of view of the gallery, but it is an actual aid in drawing the strike when the bass are looking things over rather carefully before 'doing anything rash.' It looks easy when one watches an expert rodster placing his lure in his way, and it is easy when once the knack has been acquired. But it cannot be done with a short, heavy, stiff casting rod of the old type. The rod must give with the pull of the line as the lure shoots out toward the desired spot, yet it must have backbone enough to start the plug back when the wrist gives the word. This does not mean that the bait-caster must resort to a half-breed bait-rod in order to get a good casting tool—it is more a matter of weight and calibre than of length. In nine cases out of ten the man who recommends a six to six and one-half foot light rod for bait-casting is a fly caster at heart. We have no quarrel with him whatever.

"In the majority of cases when casting for bass, a greater amount of attention could well be paid to the dive of the lure. Most bass are hooked very shortly after the bait enters the water, and it is folly to spoil one's chances by a poor placement of the offering. With the exception of the times when a splash is clearly indicated, it is the part of wisdom to ease the lure into the water with as nearly a lifelike action as is possible. Day in and day out this will get more and larger bass than the splash used indiscriminately."

In the summer of 1929 I set out to master and apply the silent dive cast. This was long before the time spinning was introduced in America and before the ¼-ounce lure marked its appearance. It was evident from the start that the key to this sort of lure entry was "the flat cast," that is, a cast with a low trajectory. With a well-timed lift of the rod tip, things worked out just as Sheridan Jones said they should. From then on I stayed with the overhead cast, reserving side-swiping for occasions when there was an obstruction to overhead casting, such as foliage or a low bridge.

A need for smaller lures led me into plug-making in the days before the ¼-ounce lure made its appearance on the American scene. Some of these homemade lures were small editions of current popular favorites, others were innovations.

When the light lure and the silent dive cast were combined, the casting equipment had to be somewhat refined if a worthy job were to be accomplished. Edward Thomas, the great rod builder of Bangor, Maine, designed and constructed for me a six-foot straight-handle split-bamboo rod that turned out to be an admirable stick for the purpose of the silent dive cast with the light lure.

When I began to use this new approach and new tackle, something interesting happened. A change took place in the nature of the strikes. The reception was now frequently spontaneous with the spat of the little lure on the water. Furthermore, the size of the fish that made these instant strikes was well above average.

The line I came to use was a soft-braid treated silk in ten-pound-test that was called "Blue Ribbon" casting line by its manufacturer, the B. F. Gladding Company. Bitter experience demonstrated that frictional wear and tear on the extremity of this fine line as it passed over the tip guide caused the first foot or so of line to weaken. This was offset by cutting away the worn portion every hour or two and retying the lure.

At that time there was on the market a Japanese synthetic gut known as Syntex, which looked like present-day monofilament but had to be soaked before it could be used. I decided to tie on about five feet of Syntex as a casting trace, thinking that it would be more friction resistant than that vulnerable last foot of braided silk. And, of course, it would also provide greater camouflage. Much to my delight, it provided both of these requirements, and something unexpected as well. It was so slick and slippery that the get-away of the plug was vastly improved, less effort was required in short casts, and long casts carried farther. This new casting ease was especially significant when I was using a light lure. Since then I have never cast a lure without using a trace.

After discovering the advantages of using a casting trace I then began to experiment with knots and with the length of the trace. The two standard leader knots of the fly fisherman, the barrel knot and the double water knot, proved satisfactory until I made another discovery. The perfect knot consisted of half of each, the braided line encompassing the double water knot and the monofilament, the barrel knot. Through the decades I have used this combination with complete satisfaction, thus proving I am sold on it.

Further trial-and-error casting determined the best length for the trace. It was perfectly clear that the knot caused no trouble, for it passed freely through the guides and also through the level-wind of the multiplying reel. Length, however, could be overdone. If the trace is too long, it has a tendency to loosen on the spool and cause a backlash at the start of the cast. A trace of nine feet or less will not do this. There is no twisted history to be unraveled in the evolution of the casting trace. That is the way it was. Its use spread over Pennsylvania as a result of publicity in *The Pennsylvania Angler*, organ of the Fish Commission, and from thence to the tournament distance casters.

Braided lines treated to float are now available. Such lines tipped out with a casting trace are superb for working skim-and-swim lures and surface lures. This combination works wonderfully well on a quadruple-multiplying reel, making possible the most enticing manipulation of the lure. Time will tell whether this line is also practical for spinning and spin-casting reels. I am not sure.

Dan Gardside had just landed a 25-pounder on a homemade Sick
Sucker given him by Charlie Fox and both were very happy about it.
Photo courtesy of Jim Bashline.

A rod must have backbone yet be resilient. This combination of qualities results in a powerful rod with quick responsiveness and comfortable lightness. A common mistake is to suppose that whippiness in a rod means good action. A soft rod is not capable of casting a lure in a low trajectory.

From the results obtained by the unofficial Possum Lake Casters' Association it must be said that there may be no single best outfit. Each fisherman will have his own favorite. It is impossible to settle every question of methods and tackle to the satisfaction of all. We must respect the other fellow's views even if we cannot agree with them.

Hooking, Playing and Landing

We hook, play, and land our fish by a combination of ingenuity and force. Each of the three steps involves a special knowledge and use of tackle. Trouble can occur anywhere along the line, but the most common failing takes place in the hooking operation. The failure of the angler to strike back with authority in answer to the strike of the fish is a hardly noticeable sort of thing, whereas the throwing of the lure by a jumping and shaking battler or the loss of a big fish during the landing operation are dramatic to the extreme.

The first requisite is sharp hooks. I have developed a useful habit that I think has so much merit that it deserves to be made known. For me, televised pro-football games provide diversion from all but one thing—hook sharpening. There I sit, watching the action with a lure in one hand and a three-sided Carborundum stone in the other. During the lineup between plays I work on hooks. About the time the offensive unit breaks out of the huddle I turn my attention from the fishing preparations to the game. Believe me, the hook points on my lures are sticky sharp.

There are two types of treble hooks, the fine bronze wire kind and the nickle kind, which are somewhat thicker. The bronze hooks are excellent for bass lures, but for muskie lures I prefer the special salt-water nickle-plated hooks.

Size is a consideration. I have friends whose judgment I respect who insist on oversize hooks, particularly for muskies. I like smaller hooks, so we argue the point. They tell me that the big hooks hold better and will not open. I tell them that it is easier to sink the barb on a smaller hook and that the bend of the small hook is completely filled when set, whereas this is not the case with the large hook. So there you have it.

How can the barbs be deeply sunk without causing damage to tackle? The vast majority of fishermen of my acquaintance retrieve the lure with the rod pointing toward it and answer the strike of the fish with a sharp, short lift of the rod. It is a snap, not a sweep or steady lift. This method works very well. It is less effective to exert constant pressure by holding the rod off to the side and continuously reeling during the course of the retrieve and directly after the strike. In the majority of cases, a bass or muskie clamps its jaws about the lure immediately after the object has been seized, and the only way the hooks can be made to move is by a jerk. In all probability, the bigger the fish, the stronger its hold. If the fish simply nips at the lure from the back, which often happens with pike and walleyes, the problem is less difficult; but most bass grasp the lure in the midsection. They snatch minnows and other food by the body, not by the tail, and the same is true of lures. The upward snap of the rod does a creditable job. If the hooks are large and not very sharp, the strike of the fish should be answered twice. The double strike is also recommended when a fish takes at the end of a long cast.

The battle of a bass for its freedom provides the beginner with his greatest fishing thrill, mainly because the outcome is always in doubt. However, as experience mounts, playing the fish becomes mechanical and the angler becomes more and more interested in the strike and what happens immediately after it. He reaches a point where he greatly enjoys the strike and attaches much significance to it while caring less and less how the hooked fish behaves and whether it escapes, unless it happens to be an exceptional specimen. He is forever on the lookout for large ones and is pretty well satisfied if the others gain freedom during the fight.

The anticipated as well as the unexpected leaps of a hooked fish are often spectacular and add variety to a phase of angling that otherwise might border on the monotonous. If the rod is held low and to the side, the fish is held down and its jumps are reduced in number and intensity; if the rod is held high, the angle of pressure encourages surface activity. In other words, the high rod increases jumping, the low rod minimizes it.

The last rays of an early September sun shimmered on the clear pocket water. The bass had been striking well all afternoon. A number had been returned, some of them good fish, others small. One big fellow was held captive in a fish bag. This was such a large bass that any additional success would have come as an anticlimax, so my attention was turned to experimentation.

The efficient Baby Popper had been tied to the leader at the start of the afternoon and it had provided so much action that I had found no reason to try another lure. As I continued to cast, a question came to mind—how long does a bass carry or hold a solid lure in its mouth before trying to eject it? Do they ever hook themselves? I decided not to answer any forthcoming strikes, but to simply let the fish take the lure and have its own way with it on a slack line, and to watch what happened. I thought the results would be of particular interest with this lure, for it was equipped with special small, bronze treble hooks, which were well honed.

The lure bobbled, floated, and plunked with the current from a cast quartering upstream. A bass snapped it under the surface, held it quietly for a few seconds, then moved nervously several yards. Suddenly the lure came to the surface. The object with the hard body and such stiff legs or fins had been ejected as unsuitable for consumption.

The next strike was of a similar type, but after the fish had held the lure for several seconds, it panicked and made a fast run against the very slight tension I placed on the reel spool. Then it jumped wildly and expelled the lure. Something had alarmed this fish as it mouthed the unusual object it had captured. Possibly the sharp hook points clung to the teeth or lips so that the object could not be turned in the mouth, as a bass is accustomed to do with its food.

At dusk the Popper disappeared in a large dimple. There was no snapping noise or broken water; the lure simply went under the surface with a minimum of commotion. About five seconds passed, and there was no apparent movement. All of a sudden the water exploded, and a very fine bass shook its head viciously as it appeared to stand on the tip of its tail. The lure flew out of its mouth and dropped about six feet away. The opportunity of taking another four-pounder was gone, and to me bass fishing is a campaign against the big ones. My experiment had placed me in such a ridiculous position that I couldn't keep from laughing out loud. But possibly a point had been proved.

These experiences and others like them, as well as numerous incidents when the answering strike was poor, all resulted in the loss of fish, which proves to my satisfaction that a bass or muskie generally gains freedom if the angler does not bring about the penetration of at least one barb. I reiterate—it is barbs that hold lures firmly, not simply the points of hooks and a line held taut by the angler.

Now and then a powerful fish straightens out one or more hooks. I believe this happens when the pressure of a power run is on the point of the hook rather than on the bend. In other words, the strike of the angler in answer to the strike of the fish did not sink the hook in to the bend.

The idea that a tight line or the spring of a rod plays out a fish is a myth; it is the fish's own activity that is exhausting, and no other escape attempt saps strength and stamina as does the jump. A spectacularly active fish does not last as long as a slow sulker. It is possible that the return to the water of a leaping fish also takes its toll, for they frequently fall back hard.

Hooking, Playing and Landing

As long as the fish is submerged it weighs nothing, for its specific gravity is about the same as that of water. When it's in its element, a hooked fish's strength or the pressure of current is felt by the angler, but the fish's weight cannot be felt. However, when the fish leaps above the surface we then contend with weight as well as a certain amount of drive and contortion. The angler should be prepared to meet the shock of jumps and should protect his tackle from this additional strain. The spring of the high-arched long rod and a gentle thumb on the spool, or the proper drag setting, will provide a sufficient margin of safety. So, in addition to encouraging jumping, the high tip protects against the hazard of strain.

Soft and gentle playing of a fish not only protects the tackle but also protects light holds of an embedded hook. Sometimes a fish is held by a mere pinch of skin that will tear if the angler employs rough tactics. One day a companion of mine had a fine pickerel snap at his plug just as he was about to lift it from the water. He could see the tail hook catch in the lip of the fish. Immediately he began to hurry and rough the pickerel, which soon parted company with him. His explanation was, "I could see that the fish was hooked lightly so I tried to get it into the boat as quickly as possible, so that it wouldn't have much time to escape." His erroneous reasoning cost him the fish, for his only chance to land that pickerel was to play it very slowly and carefully, placing as little strain on the light hold as possible, until old duckbill was too exhausted to swim.

Barring obstructions, which present their own interesting and individual problems, the idea in playing a fish is to permit it to run when it is intent on moving and to reel in line when the fish gives up or moves toward the fisherman. Light pressure is all that is necessary to keep the fish under control as it exhausts its strength. If the angler uses a reel with a level wind, it is a simple matter to exert thumb pressure on the back of the spool. If an open-face spinning reel or encased spin-casting reel is used, the drag should be set to do the job. The important thing is to thoroughly wear the fish down before attempting the landing.

Many a strong fish has gained freedom at the net. When a fish that still has some strength left first sees the boat, the angler, or the net, it makes a final desperate attempt to escape, giving the impression that it has gained a second wind. Always be prepared for this comeback.

A friend of mine who does practically all of his fishing by wading lakes and streams lost several very large bass as he was attempting to net them. He now says, "They happened to be hooked on the side of the mouth opposite from the pull of the line, and as I tried to draw them over the net, the hooks were twisted and torn out of position and they lost their holds. Now I work them in slowly and carefully until I can see exactly where the hook is embedded. Then I drag the fish over the submerged net from the hooked side so the bends of the hooks are pulling against flesh instead of being twisted backward."

When obstructions are involved, it is a case of captive and capturer, each for himself. The best the fisherman can do is to keep his head. Snags, weed, rocks, and the combination of high banks and deep water all present problems of their own. One time I had a fine bass run into a rocky tunnel from which it could not be led and from which, probably, it could not swim. I propped the rod on a nearby rock and caught the fish by hand. Another ran into a muskrat hole but backed out in about ten minutes after taking a rest. On one occasion the upstream cast carried the lure over a tree limb, and as it hit the water a bass seized it, was hooked, then played out with the help of the flexible branch. When the bass was too tired to swim very much I placed the rod on the bank, waded out, netted the fish, cut the leader, and returned to reassemble the tackle. Sometimes in rich, algae- and vegetation-laden water a hooked fish becomes completely engulfed and the whole slimy mess is brought to the net to be unwrapped. The luckiest incident I ever witnessed took place when a fellow was casting over a low barbed-wire fence into an area where trespassing was prohibited. He managed to hook a bass on the first cast which fell not far beyond the wire. The fish promptly jumped, cleared the low wire strands, and was easily captured. Working a strong, active fish out of a field of pads is like the piece by piece assembling of a jigsaw puzzle, only in this case it is a matter of pad by pad. Even anchor ropes, rotten nets, and the lines of other fishermen can create mild crises, each of which in its own peculiar way adds to the fun.

If you prefer to net your fish, go after the head first; if you like to beach them by sliding them out on a bar, lower the rod tip as you back up; if you choose to lift bass out of the water by the lower lip, using your thumb and forefinger, be sure to play them out thoroughly and be careful not to exert too much strain on the high rod as you reach for them, lest the rod snap below the tip guide.

When unhooking a bass, hold it firmly by the lower jaw with your thumb and forefinger, so that it can be carefully returned without injury. It is necessary to hold the pikes by the top of the head, above the gills. They can be lifted from the water this way. A pair of pliers is a useful implement for removing hooks.

Plastic Worms

Hendrick Van Loon wrote, "The history of man is the story of a hungry animal in search of food." To paraphrase the historian, it could be said, "The history of bass fishermen is the story of a fishing animal in search of a hunting fish." The preceding thought was prompted by a trip to Memphis, Tennessee, which might well be called the bass capital of the land. It was my good fortune to be invited to participate in the First Annual Bass Seminar and Fishing Tackle Exposition. The event was sponsored by the Arthritis Foundation and by Surplus City, a chain store, in conjunction with the bass clubs. The four-day affair was held in the elaborate Midsouth Coliseum at Memphis in June of 1972. The pleasant escapade into the beautiful South and the hospitable city was more than enjoyable; it was enlightening.

Everywhere one turned, there was bass talk and everyone wanted to talk bass. I heard much talk about fishing in twenty feet of water in the massive reservoirs and much serious dialogue about fishing with plastic worms. Soon I realized that the sport of bass fishing in the South and the sport of bass fishing in the North are two separate games. The primary job in the big deep impoundments of the Midsouth is to attempt to locate the schools of bass, then to send down a snagproof plastic worm and make it bottom crawl and hop, and when something takes it, to strike back hard. In the rivers and shallow lakes of the North we know, to a large extent, where the bass are located; the idea is to show the lure to some that are "ready" or to trigger the striking response of others. These are two entirely different ball games.

Everywhere one turned at the tackle exposition there was one variation or another of the plastic worm. There they were in various colors, sizes, and shapes, the products of various manufacturers. There were the nationally distributed Burke worms, Nick Creme's worms, and Al Reinfelder's Garcia worms. There were guides' worms and the many products of new, energetic, and enthusiastic small companies. I examined Tom Mann's Jelly Worms, Charlie Brewer's Flatheads, and Gadabout Gaddis's Glitter Worms. On display were translucent worms, opaque worms, two-tone worms, and one-tail, two-tail, floating-tail, and dragon-tail worms. Some had built-in jig heads, others had hair or rubber heads and were designed for use with the fly rod. No doubt there were other variations too. It was impressive and convincing—a sort of plastic-worm convention.

Here I learned of the many town and city bass clubs and of how and why they came into existence and who started it all. I heard for the first time of sponsored bass-fishing tournaments that involve entry fees and prize money and from which emerge titlists for future championship events.

Articulate Ray Scott, an engaging personality from Montgomery, Alabama, started it all with the formation of BASS (Bass Anglers Sportsman Society). The prosperity of this organization results from the combination of *Bassmaster* magazine, good publicity, energetic leadership, and TV exposure. At this writing the membership is about 80,000 and still growing.

At the symposium I was the babe in the woods in regard to plastic-worm fishing. All the others were experts in the field and probably pioneers. My role was that of a panelist from far away who was to talk in one session about my beloved skim-and-swim technique and in another about muskies and new waters.

The first acquaintance of mine to talk on the floor of the exposition was affable John Aldridge of Greenwood, Mississippi. He said, "We must reappraise our original thinking about how a bass takes a worm. First it was believed that they pick them up by the tail, roll them in a ball, run a short distance, then start swallowing. Everyone gave the bass lots of time, as you do when fishing with a minnow. Now we know they take them head first with suction, and therefore we can strike fast. This results in two things: first, they are not hooked deeply, so the small ones and the extra ones can be returned uninjured, having been mouth hooked, and, second, they are not given the opportunity to drop the worm, which often happens when our strike is late in coming."

One by one my path crossed those of the big winners and lecturers, and we talked plastic-worm fishing. Big Tom Mann, former warden and now a guide at Lake Eufala, Mississippi, demonstrated the hookup, then told us how he treated his worms with different flavors, such as strawberry, blueberry, and raspberry. He stated that he did not believe he had ever taken a bass in as much as thirty feet of water but had taken many in about twenty feet. Incidentally, Tom led the field in the 1971 National Tournament at Lake Mead, Nevada, and was going into the eleventh hour when his total catch was surpassed by a few ounces. First prize money was $10,000, so he jokes about how he lost ten grand at Las Vegas.

Bill Dance, of Memphis, as pleasant a person as you will ever meet, is the biggest tournament money winner, his current total being $22,000. He has secured U.S. topographical maps, made before the water was impounded, of the areas he plans to fish. From these he can locate old stream channels, wooded areas, remnants of old buildings, bridge drop-offs, and other bass cover. He makes and keeps voluminous charts. The two things he is attempting to determine are the loitering places for the schools of big bass and their passage ways back and forth from feeding grounds to resting places.

It became abundantly clear that all the pros are concerned with seeking the locations of schooled bass, and that there are great expanses of unproductive water. Roland Martin lectured on what he, and I suppose most of the southern bass fishermen, call "structure fishing." He seeks the ideal water temperature in places adjacent to cover. Pertinent equipment consists of a thermometer and a Lawrance electronic fish-finding device. He likes belts where the water temperature suddenly drops. With the electronic equipment he locates various structures at various depths. Then he combines the right temperature, which will indicate the right depth, with good cover. Once all factors are appraised, down goes the plastic worm.

These men use sturdy equipment. Lines, rod, boats, and motors are all on the husky side. The experts frequently shift location, zooming from one carefully chosen spot to another at great speeds and often over considerable distances. When a fish is hooked, it is forced up and away from the school so as not to disturb the others. Time is vital in the contests, and avoirdupois reigns supreme. The idea is to achieve the highest total weight within the daily state limit. Stringers full of bass, as well as individual big bass, have prizes on their heads. A saving grace is that many live fish are returned to the reservoirs after being registered and weighed, which places a premium on living fish instead of cheapening a great creature of nature.

Gadabout Gaddis told me how he has moved to the Saint Johns River of Florida and henceforth expects to devote his time and efforts to the protection of the environment, pollution abatement being his chief interest. When the subject turned to plastic worms, he said he likes Glitter Worms.

There were many variations in worms, but everyone advocated the weedless hookup in which the point of the single hook is run through the tip of the head of the worm, then out the neck, and after being turned half-way around, is stuck back into the body, covering the barb. A slip-on sinker is slid onto the monofilament before it is tied to the hook. Obviously the answering strike of the angler must be sharp, for the barb must be forced out of the plastic and into the hard mouth of the fish.

It was my good fortune to spend considerable time with Charley Brewer, whose fishing passions are ultralight tackle and smallmouth bass. This effervescing enthusiast is on the staff of the excellent magazine *Fishing Facts,* P.O. Box 4169, Milwaukee, Wisconsin 53210.

The tournament followers are a congenial group. They teased Bobby Meadows about not being the big winner, to which he agreed but added, "I never win, but I come in second more than anyone else." This happy guide lectured on "spinner baits," but when in competition he fishes the plastic worm. Bill Norman conducted two sessions, one having to do with fishing the clear-water lakes, the other with the design and testing of lures.

After experiencing all this, I am all for fishing symposiums and tackle expositions, particularly when staged in Memphis.

Winter Lure Fishing

It is not accurate to say that there is but one muskie winter wonderland, because the fact of the matter is there are many of them, even though few lure casters know anything about them. And furthermore, the places that are winter wonderlands for muskies are usually productive waters for bass and walleyes as well. In such places one fishes for all three at the same time. Some wonderful spots do not have muskies yet, but many could have and no doubt in due time will have. Possibly a place with such potential is located within one hundred miles of nearly everyone in the muskie belt, which is a big area. In my home state of Pennsylvania, for instance, there is a section with muskies on the Allegheny River, two on the Susquehanna, and one on the Juniata. There are two spots on the Delaware that sooner or later will harbor muskies and to the south in Maryland is another on the Potomac.

What is needed is a hydroelectric plant with a warm-water discharge. If it is built on a natural muskie river, such as the Allegheny, nature takes care of everything. If it is built where there is no native population of muskies, man must stock them as fingerlings. But let me report on the winter muskie water I think of as mine, the one that is nearest to home.

Ice does not effect the fishing in this place, because where you fish there never is any. Snow may be blowing so hard that one loses sight of the lure in its trajectory. If the line happens to freeze in the guides, it can be dipped in the river and washed free of the ice. Although the air and the ground may be frigid, you may see a painted turtle swimming around that by all odds should be hidden and stilled in deep hibernation. Sunfish and rock bass dart about, and now and then a carp porpoises. Coots are abundant, and mergansers chatter back and forth between dives. Minnows skip out of the water, indicating that a predator is on the prowl. Your hands may get cold, but if you stay in the water your booted feet won't.

At any one of these places you will be casting for smallmouth bass and walleyes, and at some, as at mine, for muskies too. The only thing that stops the fishing is the law, there being a short closed season in most if not all states. For instance, in Pennsylvania the muskie open season is from May 6 to March 14. The minimum size limit is thirty inches, and the daily creel limit is two fish. The finest fishing quarter of the year in this warm-water discharge is from mid-December to mid-March. Think of that.

"Where is this bed of roses?" you ask. "Where do you cast when the countryside is in deep freeze?" That question is particularly appropriate because my favorite spot is midway between the "white-rose city" of York and the "red-rose city" of Lancaster, within the midst of a vast population. My haven is down river from the town of York Haven.

Civilized muskies, you think to yourself. Yes, I read your thoughts, but muskies are muskies, just as bass are bass. Keep the water sufficiently clean and they don't mind civilization. Remember, this fishing is done when the resorts are closed and icebound. It is fantastic just to be able to cast into open water at this time of year, let alone to be able to hook and land game fish.

The muskies I fish over were born and raised in a hatchery and stocked when three to eight inches in length, being transported to their big river home in plastic bags. As pampered babies they taste nothing but live food, first zooplankton, then tiny minnows. Once planted in the big, rich mile-wide Susquehanna River, they acclimate themselves and wax big and strong and, it must be added, mean and temperamental. Stocking does not have to be at the plant outlet, for as game seeks and finds the comfortable provision-laden quarters, so fish do too.

The hydroelectric plant on Brunner's Island, which really isn't an island, discharges 75,000 gallons a minute of ninety-degree water, which flows 400 yards in a tailrace and thence into the Susquehanna River on the west shore opposite a large wooded island. From the standpoint of the angler, the greatness of this beautiful river is its shallowness, and at this point it is either wadable or easily boatable.

Thus this muskie winter wonderland where in the off season one can cast to his heart's content is an artificial accident. Man in his tamperings with nature usually wrecks natural environments, to the consternation of the angler and others, but, glory be, in the case of the river muskie it can work the other way, and in a big way.

For two and a half miles a band of warm water exerts its abnormal influence as it borders the western bank, slowly cooling and spreading among the big rocks. The fish choose their preferred water temperature. The catfish like it hot, so they concentrate at the head of the area, whereas the tons of carp like it a little less hot, so most of them are found downstream about a half mile. As for the muskies, they seem to prefer the very juncture of the hot and cold waters, from which they make their forays to wherever small fish can be found. It is possible that the oxygen content is the deciding factor with them, and of course this is controlled by aeration and water temperature. In the summer they are scattered over a broad range.

One day Bruce Brubaker, the national professional casting champion, and I started in downstream about two miles and worked our way up the belt. Where we first stepped in the river its temperature was sixty-seven degrees. Where we quit at the mouth of the tailrace the thermometer registered eighty-nine degrees.

For two and a half miles the river is wadable and castable.

For esthetic reasons if not for practical purposes, the fishing ends where the water from a polluted stream enters the river, causing a contaminated band that eventually disappears with dilution. Below this area the river opens up into the great pool of a dam. It is this lakelike area that supplies the heated strip with its winter muskies.

Upstream, a mile above the confluence of the heated water and the river water, is another impassable dam at a plant. Here too is some heated water, but this is deep water. On the eastern shore is a fine parking place and boat-launching ramp maintained by the Commonwealth.

The Pennsylvania Fish Commission annually stocks fingerling muskies in the large pool of the lower impoundment, the Safe Harbor Dam, and at the boat ramp of the upper impoundment, the York Haven Dam. The stockings have been substantial—as many as 12,000 muskies a year. It takes three to four years in the river for the fingerlings to exceed the legal limit of thirty inches. When six to eight years old, muskies living in this rich water, which flows through limestone country, will be big. Those that remain of the first ones stocked are over forty-five inches long and weigh more than twenty-five pounds.

It is not known yet if there is any natural reproduction here, but however wonderful it would be if this occurs, it is not vital so long as adequate fingerling stockings continue. Like the flow of the great river, the bass and walleye supply continues unabated.

It is when the broad Susquehanna is blocked with solid ice or covered with barely moving slush ice in the process of solidifying that fish move into the summerlike channel.

The body temperature of a fish is the same as the temperature of the water in which it lives, and body temperature controls the digestive process. They eat heavily and frequently in the balmy water because digestion is rapid. Here is the reverse of what the trout fisherman so often sees—the trout moving into cold water to avoid summer heat.

These fish are no pushovers. They are well fed and well educated and skill pays off. The first day I ever fished this water was on January 15, 1967. Everything was fine but the wind which blew a downriver gale. An unavoidable bow in the line developed with each cast, causing slack on the retrieve. Since the water was low, I attached the old reliable green Spark Plug, a homemade lure that pops well on top and swims beautifully in a side-to-side motion about a foot under the surface. The floater was cast quartering downstream, popped for about fifteen seconds, then ducked under for the wobbling retrieve.

After two and a half hours of pitching and slowly wading downstream, the big strike occurred from my first Susquehanna muskie. When I struck back, the bowed line ripped the water in a spray as I tried desperately to sink a barb despite the slack in the line. Power and weight were evident as the fish started up and away. The run was powerful, and as the big back showed I saw that it was a muskie and not a big foul-hooked carp. Suddenly the tension ceased. I had failed to set a hook over the barb.

I realize now, though I didn't at the time, that I was lucky to hook a January fish while pop casting with a floating plug. That is not the way it is done best at this time of year. With river muskies and walleyes wintertime is jig time, no matter whether the scene is a warm area below a power plant or a big cold-water eddy that is not frozen over. Throughout the entire winter season the jig reigns supreme, providing it is fished right. Therein lies a tale.

We turn now to the words of Tid Sheldon, a real muskie expert and the honorary president of the mythical Husky Musky Club of America. Such a switch is particularly fitting, for we are not only going to the scene of the development of this phase of lure casting but also will learn from one of the first men to use this specialized technique.

"Did any of you old-time fishermen ever have the feeling that you had fished for so many years, under such variable conditions, and in so many different lakes and streams at every season of the year that you had learned about every trick in fishing for muskies and walleyes? Had you tried all the lures, hundreds of them, as they came on the market until you had tackle boxes bulging with them? Were you always a sucker for anything new, from the rod grip at one end to the lure at the other? And then have you had your ego pierced by some insignificant little thing? That's the way it was with me a few years ago. The insignificant thing is called a jig.

"Being a resident of Crawford County, Pennsylvania, I caught my first muskie at the age of thirteen, and then in the next forty years I caught over 300 legal ones in home waters and in Ontario lakes. Crawford County, the foremost muskie county in Pennsylvania, afforded me many happy fishing hours in Conneaut Lake, Conneaut Creek, French Creek, Cussewage Creek, Edinboro Lake, and Lake LeBoeuf. Thus when I moved to Pleasantville, near the Allegheny River, I felt it would be routine to do well there.

"Directly after moving to the new town and county for my new assignment with the Pennsylvania Fish Commission, I looked up and soon became acquainted with the local muskie addicts. Every time the group collected, the conversation went something like this: "What color do you think is best?"

"White," one would answer.

"Yellow," another would say.

"Do you prefer nylon or hair?"

"Hair."

"Hair."

"Should they be three-quarter or half-ounce leads?"

"Three-quarters.

"Half."

"This sort of running patter was Greek to me. Garland Archer, the possessor of the local muskie-taking reputation, John Holtz, and Howard Levy, author of the book *Man Against Muskie*, talked nothing but muskie fishing when together, but never did they mention anything that I knew anything about. Curiosity was getting the best of me.

"Casually I asked if they would show me a yellow ½ ounce, one with hair. Archer promptly reached in a pocket and handed over a small box. My first impression of its contents was of a shaving brush, the kind Pappy used. It had a lead head, painted yellow, and a hank of yellow bucktail tied on a single hook. What a muskie monstrosity, thinks I. No doubt a smile crossed my face as I thought of the hours I had spent making plugs from carefully selected wood, cloaking them in blended paints and equipping them with treble hooks of just the right size, then testing them for the approved swimming action. When we fished together I would show them. They were not going to kid me with shaving-brush chatter.

"The November frosts hit the river country, and the foliage at the edges of the picturesque stream lit up. Archer and Holtz took me to one of their favorite eddies near the town of Tidioute. Naturally I rigged up with one of my favorite plugs and set out to show them how it is done. They could have their shaving brushes.

"I cast old faithful with my bait-casting outfit. Both Archer and Holtz broke out spinning rods with fifteen-pound-test monofilament lines and tied on their inevitable shaving brushes, which they referred to as jigs. If this is a joke, thinks I, they are carrying it pretty far.

"About the fourth cast Archer sings out, 'Fish on.' Sure enough, a walleye of about seventeen inches was brought in, only to be released with the casual remark, 'Too small.' Not long after that Holtz lets out the same battle cry. This time a twenty-seven-inch muskie was landed and released. My ego was diminishing, but I kept on casting the muskie plug. Certainly it could only be the small and ignorant fish that would strike a jig.

"Archer repeated his cry. With one glance you could see that this was something different. His rod was bent almost double, and the slip clutch on the closed spinning reel was screaming. For twenty minutes it was a battle. Although it was below freezing, there were beads of perspiration on Archer's forehead. Finally he had his fish in the big net, all forty-five and a half inches of heavy, highly-colored Allegheny 'lunge.

"I kept on casting. Nothing happened. But every so often one of the other two would yell, 'Fish on.'

"Within the next three weeks I saw fourteen legal muskies and more than thirty keepable walleyes taken on the shaving brushes, and not by these men alone, but also by Cy Sutton, Russ

Reynolds, Gordon Fogle, Cecil Toombs, Bob Parlaman, Stan Forbes, and Howard Levy.

"By this time you know I had discarded my trusty old plugs for an assortment of Archer jigs. Then the next surprise cropped up. Just because you use a spinning rod and monofilament line and cast a heavy jig a country mile doesn't mean you are going to catch fish the way the rest of them do. I found that out the embarrassing way.

"Finally I watched the others. They all fished the same lure in the same way. After hitting the water, the lure was permitted to sink to the bottom. A heave of the rod jerked it off the bottom. Four or five turns of the reel handle took up slack as the lure sank again. So the way one fishes a jig is to make it hop-toad on the bottom. Now I understood the reason for the brute fiberglass rods and the heavy lines. Most of the stones in the Allegheny are loose. If the lines are strong enough, a fouled jig can frequently be made to upset the rock and come free for the next jump off the bottom. A lot of jigs are lost when they become caught in a ledge or on submerged tree limbs, but that is part of the game. With any lures other than jigs, the cost might be prohibitive. You either mold and tie your own or buy them from Archer, three for a dollar. If you lose six in an afternoon, that isn't bad, not if some fish have been taken. Both are par for the course.

"These jumping jigs have another strange attraction. Certain fish of the river, called trash fish by the biologists, move toward these jigs to look them over. These include carp, quillbacks (silver carp), and the redhorse, a sucker. Some of these fish are hooked in the mouth, but that is not usually the case. Several fishermen may cast for an hour or two with no response, then, as if the starting shot for a race had been fired, everybody gets action—strong evidence that fish that were docile have swung into a period of activity and are attracted to the jigs.

"A big hooked carp is slow but tenacious. He won't give up, and sometimes his run may be long. The quillbacks, which usually run around one and a half pounds, are speed demons. The big red-tail suckers are a strong fish that go up to ten pounds, and some jump like bass.

"The Allegheny casters now and then smoke a big batch of carp in their special smokehouse with their preferred combination of burning woods. Smoked carp is delicious. It will make you smirk at the "planked carp" receipt. The redhorse, the "red-tail suckers," are a bag of bones, but if you cook them, put them through the old-fashioned meat grinder, which catches all the bones, and make them into fish cakes, you then have something extra special. The quillbacks are edible too."

Since Tid Sheldon wrote these words of winter muskie-fishing wisdom, he has made his jumping jigs cover many miles of Allegheny River bottom. He admits frankly that his "ego was pierced" when he learned first hand about the effectiveness of this specialized casting. He tells too how he became enamored of these hairy little lures that have no acton and but little flash and color.

Some of us, associates of Tid's in the Pennsylvania Department of Forests and Waters, have introduced the jumping jig to the fish of the Susquehanna River. It works there too in the winter, just as it does on the Allegheny.

Once the heavy frosts set in, it is time to break the rules. If you are an old-time summer lure-caster, you can't help but look aghast at the new set. Do the following remarks sound like rank heresy to you as they did to me? Forget about built-in swimming action in lures. Forget about the big-lure–big-fish theory. Forget about using a variety of lures to fool a located fish. Forget about scale finishes and sparkle. And here is the greatest paradox of all: The worse the fishing conditions appear to be, the better should be the fishing.

When the river is high and muddy the fish concentrate in the eddies along the bank. When the river was low, Tid showed me exactly where he hooked the prize-winning Allegheny River muskie for 1966. The spot was up on a man's lawn when the river was wild. The fish took the jig in two feet of water, then waged its battle among the flotsam and jetsam in the middle of the river. When the ice is breaking up and flowing, both muskies

The father-and-son Fox team getting organized for some fall fishing.

and walleyes head for the shorelines, particularly to the eddies and the mouths of small streams.

My favorite winter-fishing environment is the warm water below a hydroelectric plant, but there are times and places when river jig fishing can be pursued away from these artificial environments. I am sure that for many a lure-caster the concept of winter jig fishing could open the door to a wonderful new fishing experience, just as it did for Tid Sheldon and I, thanks to Archer, Levy, Holtz, Parlaman, and the Allegheny Jig Casting Society. Truly it seems unlikely, but the fishing is fantastic nonetheless.

Reflections

When is the best time to fish? This is a question commonly asked by those who attempt to choose the most opportune hours in their pursuit of game fish. The answer of the inveterate angler is, whenever possible. He likes to quote the proverb, "Allah does not deduct from the allotted time of man those hours spent in fishing." This question of when to go is unimportant to the intensive angler but is all important to the one who is forced by circumstance to carefully choose his limited time. We have all learned from experience that some times are more productive than others, a condition that brings about thought, experimentation, and hope.

During the heat of the bass season, I prefer the last hour of daylight. This is the time most of the aquatic insects hatch, and their presence sets other living creatures into action. The small fish feed on the minute organisms, and the large fish turn on the small ones. It is the time when the better fish come out of hiding and go on the prowl. Quiet water often becomes alive; we see more surface activity, and we receive more strikes. This charmed hour of the summer evenings is so interesting to me that I rarely miss one, feeling that such a loss is ill afforded. For me, the last hour has been the best hour so far as consistent action and big fish have been concerned, particularly when it is calm and there is a brilliant sunset.

As the season wanes and frosty nights supplant warm ones, the better fishing occurs earlier in the afternoon. The warmth of the sun at this time feels good to the angler and apparently it is appreciated by the game fish as well.

It is commonly accepted that fish do not take well and insects do not hatch in profusion when the barometer is falling. Apparently the lower forms of life feel normal under constant rising pressures, but falling pressure has an effect that puts fish off their feed. When the silvery undersides of foliage appear, the angler can be certain that the glass is dropping and precipitation is pending.

My favorite time is the clearup after a thunderstorm, when pressure is rising. The largest trout I ever caught, which happened to be one of a great catch, was taken before dusk after a noisy midafternoon thunderstorm but before the water had clouded too much for fly fishing. It happened at a place I have fished many times, before and since, but it was the finest fish and the finest catch this place had produced for me. I gave the credit to the effect of the storm. That was some years ago. After this incident, I was eager to be at excellent spots under similar conditions on both bass and trout water.

One mid-August afternoon, there was a thunderstorm, and before the storm had abated I made my way to a spot on the Conodoguinet Creek where I knew there was a good number of bass, some of them big ones. I waited in the car about half an hour until the clouds broke and the rain, which had not been hard enough to silt the stream, had ceased falling.

I attached to the leader a Shakespeare Midget Spinner in its brightest version—yellow body and red head—and started to fish, quartering downstream in this relatively slow stretch of flat water. One good, solid, jolting strike after another was received. There was none of that chasing of the lure and nipping at it; the bass went after it and took it quickly as though they really meant business. The average size of the fish was good. Bass after bass was unhooked and slipped back into the stream. I was hoping for and expecting the big one on each cast. I had become so deeply engrossed in this interesting fishing that the voice that came from behind me was startling.

"I see you are cashing in on the storm." It was an old friend, Rex Radle, who was a confirmed fly and spinner man and the best I have ever seen with the heavy fly rod and clumsy lures. "I've been watching you for half an hour as I fished my way downstream and I'm finally convinced that plugs will do a good job. That business appears to be interesting enough to warrant a fair trial. How about selecting an outfit for me?"

In the years to come, Rex became highly efficient with the casting rod, and it was a disappointment to me when he moved from our region to Philadelphia. Rex was one of the few fishermen of my acquaintance who always headed streamward during an afternoon thunderstorm to take advantage of the fine fishing that so often accompanies the clearup. His faith in this condition increased my own confidence in it, and from that day in the early thirties I have made every effort to be on a good piece of bass or trout water at the conclusion of an electrical storm. Credit what you will—high barometric pressure, rising water, decrease in water temperature, or aeration from large driving raindrops, possibly all of these elements—this is the best time of all to be out fishing.

Long trips to fine, inaccessible waters are great. The scenery, the abundance of fish, the company, the camp life, the shore dinners are all highly desirable, but such trips come too infrequently, and they seem to be so short-lived. There was a time when this, to me, was the essence of fishing, but I have come to cherish even more those evenings along the water after the office closes. I now look forward from one evening to the next with just as keen anticipation and delight as was formerly the case with long trips. If I had to give up one or the other, it would not be the evening fishing in home waters. Fortunate indeed is the man who lives beside or within convenient striking distance of clean water, for clean water and game fish are inseparable.

All things are governed by the laws of relativity. Which does an angler appreciate more, a big fish from nearby hard-fished water or one of equal size from distant, virgin territory? Which produces the greater amount of satisfaction, the ultimate landing of a spectacular battler from a complicated place, or the catching of a slow, weak fish from open water? Do we prefer to hear a friend describe how he located a fine shy fish, on various occasions tried to catch it, and was ultimately successful in taking the fish by smart angling, or do we prefer to hear how someone landed one after another as fast as he could pull them in? Unquestionably every fisherman reacts the same to these questions. The frame of mind of the angler has a great deal to do with his enjoyment of his sport and his appraisal of success. Each one of us sets his own standards, which vary with environment. If this adjustment did not come naturally, we would all feel discontented unless we thought we were in the very best section of the very best water. It is not the most or the biggest fish that call us back, although these are factors; it is something much greater, more deeply rooted.

Interest is not held by past accomplishment; it thrives on what might take place in the future, on the next trip, on the next day, on the next cast. Anglers do not live in the past; they live in the future. That is why the urge to get out is so strong. During the progress of a day's fishing, one derives a certain amount of satisfaction and pleasure from the knowledge that he has fished the water well, and conversely he is dissatisfied when he knows that he has made a shambles of his efforts.

I despise competitive fishing in which one man is trying to put it over another by showing the most dead fish at the day's end. It turns a clean, wholesome sport into an exercise in greed where the best water is hogged and fish that should have been returned are killed. Bad fishing spoils good water. Good manners, conservation, thoughtfulness, and artistry are all a part of angling.

The late Fred Everett, the renowned wildlife artist, once told me that to get the greatest enjoyment out of his angling he refrains from going forth with men whose angling does not meet with his approval or with strangers whose ethics are unknown to him. He told me of an occasion when he played caddie to a certain individual, taking him to a particularly fine place, showing him what to do, giving him the right lure, and insisting that he fish the best spots at the best times. Under Fred's expert tutelage this individual caught fish, all of which were promplty killed. Later he had the audacity to boast about his brilliant performance and how he had beaten the expert at the expert's own spot, not appreciating one iota how Fred had gone all out for him to make the trip a productive and memorable occasion.

If ever a man should be careful of the company he keeps, it is when he is fishing or hunting. Life is too short and trips too few to have any of them marred. Paradoxically, though, 'the sport is a great equalizer. The most skilled, the most interested, the smartest, and often those possessing a degree of sportsmanship that is a delight to see can and do come from both sides of the railroad track. They may gain their livelihood with their heads or their hands, they may be affluent or they may struggle for a meager existence. What has developed more beautiful friendships and closer ties than angling and hunting friendships, which on the surface might seem odd but which, in reality, are so very natural? I have known fishing and hunting teams of judge and chauffeur, preacher and prize fighter, executive and laborer. The manner in which a so-called sport and guide so frequently take to each other is a common example. Who said that it is politics that makes the strangest of bed fellows?

But there is a peculiar circumstance in connection with these sports. Some highly respected citizens, whose integrity is generally beyond reproach, may not be able to resist the temptation of beating the limit or taking something out of season. There are people who cheat under only one circumstance, and that is when they are in quest of creatures of nature. On the other hand, some character of questionable repute may cherish his sport, fish and hunt cleanly, and spend time and money in an honest effort to assist a faltering conservation even when he knows he will never hunt or fish at the improved spot. Unfortunately, not everyone gets out of hunting and fishing what they put into it or what they deserve.

A taint on the sport is the fact that all too frequently these two types, the 100-percent sportsman and the cheat, are thrown together on the stream or in the field, although, when given a choice, sportsmanship seeks its own level. The situation in which people who think differently are placed in competition with each other was the main reason that open hunting and fishing as we know them in America disappeared in England and some of the countries of the Continent before the turn of the century. The hope in the United States is that the ranks of the law abiding, the interested, and the courteous are increasing as the greedy and the inconsiderate decrease in number. The greatest obligation of the outdoor writer is to make an honest effort to educate the participants in the outdoor sports, particularly the neophytes, along two lines, namely, ecology and ethics. A public that is ignorant, ill-mannered, or ill-advised as to what is needed to perpetuate a sport could seal the doom of open hunting and fishing.

The best of the fishermen I have met have been thoughtful and analytical, taking little for granted and frequently challenging the generally accepted practice. Conditions vary from area to area and fluctuate from time to time, so that generalities mean little and are misleading. Bear in mind that the heavy plug made its reputation when it was still legal to fish during the spawning season, a period when the protective instinct of bass guarding eggs and fry prompts them to smash anything that appears to threaten the welfare of their offspring.

One time I saw a male bass guarding a nest in the creek below our house. A young friend fishing nearby with worms spied it and was immediately interested in catching it. Upon my request, he handed over his cut pole with a sturdy line tied to the end. I removed the hook. From our concealed position behind a bush on the bank I lowered the sinker toward the nest. The bass moved forward, grasped it in its mouth, and carried it away from the nest. When dropped by the bass, the sinker swung back and over the nest. Again the conscientious parent carried it away. When the sinker was drawn rapidly across the nest, the bass made a vicious strike that jerked the pole. My young friend saw and learned the role in life of the male bass after his mate has deposited eggs in their nest. His interest and respect for the fish were profound. Once he understood the situation, he would no more have thought of harming such a fish than he would have considered injuring a mother bird on the nest.

One day late in May I fished my way to the mouth of a trout stream. In view of the fact that things were not very interesting, I looked over the bass water in the big creek below the outlet of the spring stream. In the shallows directly above some deep ledge water was a clean-looking bass nest. Finally, I picked out the mottled, well-camouflaged form of the guardian bass, a two-pounder. Being tired, I sat down and watched the fish. Three carp swam leisurely toward the shallow water in the direction of the nest. When they approached within twenty feet, the bass saw them. He cruised around the nest, then assumed a position between them and the nest. Suddenly he charged the carp. There was a great swirl, and all three carp turned downstream and made for the safety of the deepest part of the flat. The bass had jabbed an erected and bristling dorsal fin into the underside of one of the carp. They could not possibly compete with such a speedy, formidably equipped warrior. A plug the size of a fifteen-pound carp would then probably have taken that bass.

Back in the 20s Bill Vogt, professional entertainer, trick caster, and author of the book *Bait Casting,* conducted a one-man campaign to prevent fishing for bass on the spawning beds. To prove to the public that such fish were at the mercy of the anglers and needed protection at this time of year, he indulged in fish-catching exhibitions in certain Florida lakes. One day he caught and returned 835 largemouth bass and on the succeeding day took and released 756.

Fishermen and conservation departments finally realized that the supply of male bass would be depleted under heavy fishing pressure at this time of year if protection were not provided. No lure designed by the hand of man and no legal fishing method could capture bass in such quantitites except during the spawning season. It is little wonder that some lures developed reputations of being killers, yet the fact of the matter is they were limited in their efficiency to a brief period under a very definite circumstance. Unquestionably some of these lures were well made and properly designed, but they were all large and heavy—too large and too heavy to compete with their ¼-ounce counterparts fished during the summer.

Furthermore, there is another short period when the females are vulnerable to fishing pressure. Before the deposition of the eggs, during the last days of their development, the heavy females will strike slow-moving, easily captured targets. Here again, the first large plugs took their toll and made their reputations, and here again protection was imperative if the harvest was to stay within the bounds of the natural surplus.

The best testing time for a lure is the summer and fall, and the best testing ground is low, clear, warm water, for these are the conditions under which we do a great deal of fishing. It is under these conditions that the ¼-ounce lure comes into its own.

Lures and their finishes fall into two general categories, attractors and deceivers, and most are in the former classification. Bright colors are often attractive to bass, yet lures decorated in this manner could hardly look like natural food. I believe that the brightest lures are at their best early in the season, after the bass have left the beds, when they are hungry, pugnacious, and inclined to move for food. The brightly colored lures are also the natural choice for cloudy water.

By mid-July, I prefer to switch to scale finishes and somber colors for underwater lures. I have not been able to determine whether color makes much difference in surface lures, but I am convinced that it does with those that are submerged. A sound combination is low, clear water and natural, dull finishes.

One of my favorite colorations is varnished red cedar. It has a deep, rich color broken by fine grains. We use many such homemade lures. Some small blocks of cedar are two-toned. It is a simple matter to work such a piece of wood on a lathe so that the underside or belly of the lure will be a dirty yellow and the back a dark brown. We call it "the catfish finish," and it is in harmony with nature's color scheme, light on the bottom and dark on the back. My favorite finish for the little underwater propeller lures is dark cedar dipped in lacquer in which fine bright-green metal powder has been mixed. The color of such a lure is shiny dark brown with a delicate green sheen. My best bass of one season was taken from big broken water on one of these little torpedoes with 4/0 Pflueger propellers. This was a rugged twenty-one inch smallmouth bass that weighed four and a half pounds. This particular finish is a favorite of Gene Benner, who was the first to mix the concoction to be painted on the homemade lures.

There is a definite relationship between the speed of the retrieve of an underwater lure and the clarity of the water. The vision of the fish is sharper in clean, unsilted water than it is in water that carries visible particles of suspended silt. Experience indicates that the better the fish can see, the more particular they become. Frequently they carefully inspect a slow-moving lure by swimming leisurely behind it; then when satisfied they do not want to eat it, they turn away. These are interested fish that could be hooked. Had they been presented a fast-traveling lure at the same level, the chances are good that they would have seized it for examination rather than scrutinized it at their leisure and at their chosen distance. When a fish can be seen following a lure, it can generally be induced to strike if the speed of the retrieve is quickly increased, then decreased. The fish darts forward as the object appears to be attempting escape, then when the speed of the retrieve is checked, the momentum of the fish carries it into the lure and the fish usually strikes as the two come together.

It is something of a problem to bring about a relatively fast retrieve at a low depth. One friend had a highly successful Canadian trip when he employed for the most part a scale-finish Go-Deeper River Runt and the fast retrieve. For ten days he caught large- and smallmouth bass and pike with regularity throughout the hot days. In the evening he switched to surface lures, his favorite being the Jitterbug, but it was the deep-running, relatively fast-traveling daytime lure that made the trip so interesting to him.

The combination of depth and fast retrieve can be attained in a stream by casting a sinking lure crosscurrent or slightly downstream, at first permitting the lure to gain depth, then swimming it into action through the desired spot. The swing of an underwater lure in current is attractive to bass and the pikes just as the arc in the course of a streamer fly's progress is effective on trout.

There are two excellent pockets in the Susquehanna River that I periodically fish. Both are deep, quiet holes protected by steep ledges at the heads. Both can be fished from just one side of the river. Long casts slightly up and across the stream make it possible to swing a lure at any desired depth through the best part of the holes. Each is a spot where bass loiter by day in the heat of summer and congregate in schools in the late fall, there to spend the winter. In the summer these bass will take a fast-traveling lure that passes diagonally downstream through the hole. In the fall, a lure cast directly downstream from the ledge at the head, then drawn very slowly upstream, is usually effective.

Both large- and smallmouth bass are grand game fish, and it is foolish to regard one as being better than the other. Each has its place, each has its special merits. The largemouth is the more consistent striker of the two, and the smallmouth is stronger and capable of greater power runs and more brilliant surface jumps. The largemouth prefers to operate around weed beds, whereas the smallmouth prefers clean stone. The largemouth is basically a warm-water fish; the smallmouth thrives in a cooler environment. All of these lines are frequently crossed, yet there is no conflict between the two. We are fortunate to have both.

It is claimed by some that large bass do not put up so spectacular a fight as the two- and three-pounders. My experience, with but one exception, has been that the bigger they are, the rougher and stronger they are. The comparison is like that between prize fighters—a good big man is tougher than a good little man. I have had two big bass jump completely out of water ten or more times and two other big ones that ran deep into the backing. These four bass were smallmouths from four to five and a quarter pounds. No two- or three-pounders have approached these performances. That first jump and that first run of a big bass are two of the greatest thrills of the fresh-water angler.

The large bass furnish the cream of bass fishing. Like reptiles but unlike mammals, all fish grow until death; therefore the big ones are the old, shy specimens. The very existence of such fish is one of the great appeals of the waters we fish. To many they constitute the essence of angling, and so long as some can occasionally be interested in lures, nothing else matters too much.

The angler should make a study of lures, determine which ones are best for given circumstances, and learn how each should be retrieved. A lure may be highly effective as used by one fisherman but in the hands of another may not be nearly so attractive to game fish.

"Look what Mr. Brooks and I caught," says Susie Fox.
Photo by Joe Brooks.

Recollections

For two seasons following a series of successful Canadian trips that had produced their share of what might be termed trophy fish, I fished long, hard, and often around home without so much as touching a big bass with hand or hook. That was in a time when there were many more fish than we have today, including a considerable number of large ones. I could see them and even hear them, but I was not able to induce a single one to strike. There were too many unsolved problems, and I did not know what to do. I looked forward to catching a big bass from home waters with as keen anticipation as I did to shooting a buck, making a double on birds, or capturing a large trout—none of which I had accomplished up to that date but all of which are now recorded in pleasant memory. During the years following those two seasons, after I had gained a more thorough understanding of effective plug fishing, my average was about twenty four-pounders a season along with lesser fish in greater numbers than were previously taken.

The circumstances surrounding my first big bass from hard-fished waters were unusual and made the catching of it more interesting and the memory of it more vivid. On the Fourth of July, 1932, Lew Kunkel and I fished the Conowago Creek. I was at least one hundred yards below Lew and on the

Ted Williams caught this muskie on a fishing trip to South Twin Lake, Wisconsin, following the '48 baseball season. Photo courtesy of Wisconsin Natural Resource Dept.

opposite side of the stream when I saw a large bass barely under the surface, resting in sunlight directly beside shaded water. The fish appeared to be motionless. The chances were great that a cast would be so startling to the exposed bass that it would immediately run for cover, and I wanted Lew to see this sight, so I refrained from casting and called for him to join me. The tone of my order, "Come here," must have aroused his curiosity, for he hurried, a pace unusual for Lew.

We admired the fish from a conservative distance and from the cover of some bushes; then Lew insisted that I make a cast. At the time I was using an Al Foss Shimmy Wiggler with a nickel finish and white bucktail. The lure landed in the water about fifteen feet above and beyond the fish. The retrieve had hardly started when the bass shot forward and viciously intercepted the lure. I could see the lure in the mouth of the fish before the strike could be felt. When the hook was set, the bass was jerked sideways and the gills were extended. It shook itself like a dog but did not break the surface. The subsequent run of over one hundred feet carried into the filler line and the knot passed into the water. Since that time, I have seen this happen with only three other bass. At the conclusion of the run the fish jumped twice. This practically exhausted its strength, and I reeled it to our feet and Lew netted it.

Much to our surprise there were terrible scars on both sides of the dorsal fin, which were almost completely healed. Some sharpshooter with a gig had hit his mark but none of the three wide prongs happened to sink into a vital part. The smallmouth had fed well enough to regain strength and weight, and apparently its convalescence included sunlight treatments.

Nestled in Idlewild Park on the outskirts of Pittsburgh is a fine little pond inhabited by largemouth bass and pickerel. The water is clean and rich, and the perfect balance of nature is maintained there, for the pond is open to public fishing on only one day each year, and therein lies a story. Annually the local sportsmen's clubs and the park management conduct a live-fish contest that attracts wide attention and in which the many participants compete for prizes. It is quite an event, for the competition is keen and the awards are cherished. These Pittsburgh fishermen are different from any others I have ever met. Their waters are running sores, ruined by pollution, and as a result these men derive an unusual amount of pleasure from competitive angling, casting events, and artificial fishing that would not be too well received in clean, open country. They take it as a matter of course that half their recreational time reserved for angling is spent traveling to and from clear water.

Bill Nichol, who resides on a farm near the park, had his eye on the forthcoming event. He was of the opinion that the right lure fished in the proper manner should produce, and so far as he was concerned, it was worth time and energy to attempt to work out the best possible procedure. He traveled to the other end of the state to see his old friend Jim Kell, and there the three of us fished together. Bill thoroughly explained the problems presented at the live-fish contest; he described the contour of the pond and specified what aquatic life thrived therein. The questions in his mind were, What lure should he employ, how should he fish it, and where should it be cast? At first Jim and I joked about his enthusiasm for this brief chance at what might be action-packed competitive fishing and at his description of how the fishermen lined up poised to bombard the pond at the given signal, but soon we were all equally interested in the problems involved.

A plan of attack was formulated as follows: first of all, the lure should be small and light in weight and should be cast so that it hit the water flatly and with as little commotion as possible. It should be an underwater lure. The Midge Oreno was chosen. This would probably be the only lure employed there that would have a good chance of taking fish directly after it touched the water. The finish, we felt, should be a close imitation of the natural food of this pond, so the South Bend green scale was chosen. The Midge was to be cast as much as possible to water that had not been disturbed by the heavy splashes of large lures. The idea was to cast to fish that had not been startled or made suspicious. A casting leader would be employed to facilitate casting and to add camouflage.

The day of the event arrived and passed, and the news of the result traveled eastward. Bill Nichol won everything in the lure-casting event as well as the grand prize for the day. He caught the first bass, the largest bass, the largest pickerel, and the most fish. It was the first time in the history of the event that a clean sweep had been made. The combination of good management and the smile of Dame Fortune was invincible.

The telephone rang and the cheerful voice on the other end of the line was that of Alex Sweigart, editor of the *Pennsylvania Angler*. He said that his friend Baird Hershey, a taxidermist at the state museum, wished to secure a big bass for the purpose of mounting. Strangely, there was no such thing in the state collection. It would be a hand-painted papier-mâché mount made from a mold, and it would be done in duplicate so that the man who supplied the fish would be the recipient of a reproduction. It was a Friday afternoon, and Alex was advising some of the fellows of this request in the hope that a suitable fish would be produced promptly. Here was a challenge and an interesting sort of proposition.

I knew where there were two fine bass in a rather small ledge pocket, either of which would qualify as a fine museum specimen. A heat wave accompanied by drought was in progress, so it seemed advisable to concentrate on night fishing. "Hope springs eternal in the human breast." I wanted one of those bass. I wanted it badly, and I thought I could get one over the weekend.

About nine-thirty Saturday evening I slipped into casting position. Distant flashes of heat lightning periodically illuminated the stream, so that it was possible to obtain quick glimpses of the protruding ledge that was directly below the pocket where I had seen these fish the previous week. From my position to the side and slightly above the pocket, the Baby Popper could be cast into the hole, a distance of about eighty feet, and fished slightly against the current, thus producing the best possible popping action and noise. The lure had been especially equipped with bronze hooks, so that if a strike was forthcoming from one of those fish, I would have the best possible chance of sinking the hooks.

The light spat of the lure and the popping sound that followed were just right. There were successive flashes of lightning as the lure passed over the best part of the water. Nothing happened. The sky remained dark during the progress of the next retrieve. There is great tension when one is concentrating on his angling and doing the best he can over the known position of a fine fish. Suddenly anticipation was substantiated by a noisy eruption of the water. I snapped the rod upward, and it arched and throbbed in response to a heavy live weight. The fight that ensued was rough and noisy. Eventually a tired bass was slid out of the water and onto a sand bar. I knew it was big, and I felt sure it was one of the fish I had previously located. When I placed my hand on it in the darkness and felt the broad side, I knew I had a fish of well over four pounds. Three and a quarter pounds would not have been enough; anything over four pounds was satisfactory. Elated, I turned homeward with pleasant thoughts in mind.

On Monday morning I arrived at the museum with my prize carefully wrapped in a wet towel. Baird Hershey would be pleased and surprised to know that he could be supplied so promptly with a fine specimen. As I approached the workshop, I could see a group of people, among whom were Alex Sweigart, Baird Hershey, and Lloyd King. They were in a huddle, apparently examining something. It looked fishy. As I approached, Alex jubilantly proclaimed, "Look at this. Lloyd brought in a bass for Baird."

Before them was a real one, all twenty-two inches, five pounds, ten ounces of him. It came from the Juniata River, taken at dusk on a Jitterbug. Lloyd explained that he had previously located the fish and had taken it exactly where he figured it to be.

Alex noticed something under my arm. "What's that?"

"Oh, just a package," I replied casually and turned to leave.

"They don't wrap things in towels," he said and relieved me of my burden. By comparison with the museum specimen, my fish was insignificant.

If by chance the following little yarn falls into certain hands, some young men may learn the answer to an old riddle, possibly one of a haunting nature. The August night was dark and filled with the strange noises of nocturnal insects. To my left was a line of low-hanging trees on an abrupt bank, and just beyond them was a peculiar tower that served some purpose for the geological survey. To my right was smooth ledge water, good night water. I stood thigh deep beneath a dark canopy of arched branches under which I could cast the Peanut Jitter Bug. I had carefully waded to this spot, and I was standing quietly in the water until the temporary ill effects of ripples on the surface would be forgotten by the bass.

Thin voices approached. A group of boys had left their tents and their scout master some one hundred yards distant to explore the tower. Their sight was limited to the small area illuminated by a failing flashlight. Immediately a noisy debate ensued as to who was to climb the metal ladder that led to the top of the tower. One boy dominated the group. His changing voice was directed at the fellow he addressed as "Tubby," who he thought should climb the ladder. Tubby, in soprano tones, claimed that he wasn't afraid but did not see why he should be the first to go up. Dares and counterdares were freely exchanged. Tubby was not going to be talked into anything, and apparently no one else was either. They had no idea that the controversy was being held within twenty-five feet of unknown human ears.

I cast the surface bait into the darkness, but its gurgle could not be heard above the crescendo of voices. Suddenly, explosively, there was a terrific surface commotion.

"Whatzat?" demanded the owner of the crackly voice.

All was again silent except for the katydid chorus. A big bass had been hooked. In a few seconds there was a jump that created another great eruption.

"That can't be a fish," says one.

"Must be the bull," answers another.

Again silence was followed by aquatic chaos.

"Let's get out of here," proclaimed the crackly voice, and at that they stampeded.

The last I heard was an imploring cry, "Wait for me, fellows." It sounded like Tubby.

No one reached the top of the tower, at least not that night; a big bass had taken care of that.

Vince Marinaro, the author of the classic *A Modern Dry-Fly Code,* is not only the most sophisticated angler I have ever met, he is also the finest dry-fly man for trout I have ever accompanied on a stream. Time and again, when we have been out together, he has demonstrated his ability and resourcefulness. This wielder of the magic fly rod is also the possessor of sharp eyes that not only are attracted by movement but can also penetrate water. At the conclusion of each trout season he feels rather sick and has a hopeless air about him, as though he has been deserted and can see that there will be no future. He indulged in some bass bugging, probably because it reminded him of his beloved trout angling, but every time I mentioned plug fishing he either snorted with contempt or politely reminded me not to be obtrusive.

The day finally came when we went to a bass stream together. The watershed we visited is in the glacial area, and the stream is littered with slippery, round rocks from the size of an ostrich egg to that of an igloo. The water was low and clear.

Time after time Vince worked his way into the stream toward a strategic casting point only to slip and slide, causing wakes to roll over the water. His feet would get too wide apart, and as the splitting tendency intensified, he would drop his free hand on a submerged rock to hold on and get his balance. A human in the position of a tripod knee-deep in water and with rear part sagging presents a ridiculous figure. Each pocket in turn was temporarily ruined by the rings of the water generated by slipping and sloshing boots. Vince was having difficulties.

In the meantime I walked on the sand bars and the bank and waded in the shallow weed beds, flicking a light lure the required 90 to 120 feet, to the interesting pockets in the deeper water where the bass were located. Had Vince known that this was by design, not accident, that he had been deliberately led to such a complicated spot for bass bugging, a great friendship might have terminated.

Vince became tired and was undoubtedly footsore and discouraged, so he sat down on a convenient boulder. From this spot I was in his view. The wet wading at the edge of the stream was easy, and the old hunting boots and woolen trousers were comfortable. I eased along the shore line, casting a little propeller lure to the sides of undermined boulders and grass patches and into the deeper pockets, and no waves crossed the quiet water. I caught several bass in the water Vince had fished the preceding hour. The last of these was eighteen inches in length, a good fish for this stream.

Vince was definitely interested and possibly impressed. When I sat down on an adjacent rock, he examined the trim six-foot rod and the light line with the long nylon trace. I opened the kit containing the lures. He examined them and was surprised at their small size and light weight.

"Go ahead and make a cast," I suggested.

As he walked to the nearby sand bar, he explained that for several seasons he had done some plug casting, but it was with a short, stout rod, and heavy line, and lures weighing ¾ of an ounce. He had not liked it, so he gave it up. The sort of equipment he now held was new to him. The old feel of the thumbing of the reel came back, and he had no trouble with the casting.

In surprise he explained. "These little lures with this tackle can be cast as well as big lures on heavy tackle. Let's see how close I can come to the log over there." He was fascinated by the casting, and he easily and quietly worked his way along the banks as he tried to hit various marks across the way.

I knew then that another convert had been made and that I had been vindicated of being a practitioner of a crude art.

Since that day some years ago Vince has built his own six-foot-six-inch rod, an exceptionally fine casting tool, has made and purchased an excellent assortment of lures, and has spent many enjoyable hours at this new-found game. No longer does he undergo a period of mourning at the expiration of every trout season. This particular conversion is cherished by me more than the landing of my best fish; it remains my greatest angling victory.

The three Lower boys were a colorful and successful angling triumvirate, but it was Elmer who was the enthusiastic pioneer who showed the way to the other two. Of the three, I knew him best, and we became close personal friends and periodic fishing companions. He was a kind man with a great personality and the possessor of an astute business mind. I was in his restaurant on its opening night under his stewardship, when he did not possess enough money to make change for customers, and I watched his business grow and flourish until he was financially independent, a situation brought about mainly by his personality.

He and I entered into a gentlemen's agreement. In view of the fact that we were both interested in large bass and fished the same spots, we agreed to tell each other of any big fish that we located and to be explicit in regard to location, feeding habits, stream bottom, and any other pertinent knowledge that was gathered. It was a sort of two-man campaign. In reference to the many fishing friends who were his patrons, he said, "We'll double-team them and catch more big bass. Then I will pour it on." He attached greater significance to big fish than any man I ever met. His creed was, "Concentrate on the big ones, and if you are good enough to catch a few of them, you will catch plenty of little ones; return all but the biggest."

One evening about an hour after dark I stopped at the restaurant to get supper, as was my general custom throughout the trout and bass season. Elmer slipped over to the corner of the bar where I was located and confidentially advised, "At the head of the Plumb, twenty-five feet below the large submerged rock, there is one that will go over four pounds. I lost him this afternoon through carelessness. Had him hooked on a Midget River Runt but I got over anxious when he was in close and the hook tore out. It ripped the left side of the mouth; I could see that."

About a week later I paid the spot a visit. I speculated that if the bass had been injured as badly as Elmer thought, it would do little or no feeding for about five days, after which it would be both ravenous and reckless.

To make a short story shorter, a trim bass that had a bad tear on the upper part of the left side of its mouth was taken on a slow, deep-traveling Yellow Sally Minno-Bug. It weighed four and a quarter pounds. Both Elmer and I were convinced that it was his fish. Because of the odd circumstances, I mounted the head of this fish, which on occasion serves to remind me of a great fellow with whom I had so many happy times.

One year Jim Lower outdid the best efforts of his loquacious brother. The Harrisburg Hunters and Anglers Association, one of the largest sportsmen's clubs in the country, conducts an annual big-fish contest in which the prize fish are determined by length not by weight, a practice that in theory keeps the game honest. Jim caught a smallmouth bass that measured a little better than twenty-one inches in the Susquehanna River, about one mile from his home and about six miles from Harrisburg. He held the fish temporarily in a live bag, tied it in a convenient spot, then drove home for a wash boiler. He then transported his fish alive to the Harrisburg Hardware Store, where entries are made for the contest. As soon as the official measuring was completed, he rushed his fish to the place of capture and released it. Jim absorbed a lot of ribbing as the result of this, the main theme being that he planned to re-enter the fish in the contest after its re-capture at a later date, when its growth had increased.

Incidentally, he had a winner.

About a week before the bass season was to open I was looking over prospects. In the cool water below the mouth of a trout stream was a fine pocket adjacent to an island. There in the shallows of a willow I saw a very large smallmouth bass. He was beautifully proportioned, and the mottled cloak of the spawning season was still in evidence. The water was so clear that I could watch his every move. A large dragonfly darted toward the location and hovered over the water. The great bass moved to within striking distance. As the position of the insect changed, the fish moved with it. Would such a fish lunge out of water to capture a fly? The question remains unanswered, for the dragonfly departed. I reported the location of this fish to Elmer and assured him it was all of five pounds.

There was a driving rain before the opening day, which silted the stream; nevertheless, the fishermen turned out in full force at the appointed time. The first news I got that night at the restaurant was that Harry Lower had caught the largest bass taken in the area and had taken it from discolored water on the smallest casting size Red Eye Wiggler.

Elmer Lower slipped over to me. "Harry caught your fish," he confided. "You know how it is. I had to tell him about it. After what Jim did last year, Harry needed some encouragement. Now I'll tell you where there is another just as big."

And so it went around New Cumberland, Pennsylvania, in the years preceding Pearl Harbor, always something interesting, often something spectacular.

Sweet sounds to the ears of the bass fishermen are those of surface-feeding fish. A tone of basso profundo proportions is produced by the possessor of plenty of heft and a big maw, whereas the thinner, higher tones are made by his lesser brethren. To the one for whom angling is an obsession, a series of such watery glumps is more stirring than the notes of the *Moonlight Sonata*.

No doubt you have fed scraps to the dog and associated the noise he makes as he snatches them with the sound of surface-feeding fish. In our home the dogs are spoiled, for we feed them at the table. The cocker sounds like a fourteen-inch bass, the setters like four-pounders. Recently, as Old Jeff snapped up the last scrap of meat, my thoughts turned to a lake in the mountains.

The beauty of a natural body of water, like that of a gem inlaid in an appropriate setting, enjoys universal appreciation, but there are bodies of water other than natural lakes that do not possess beauty in such abundant supply but which are more precious to the angler because they contain many protruding stumps. I am one who will sacrifice beauty for better fishing, but just to a small degree. I refuse to angle among tin cans, submerged tires, and dead chickens.

I was thinking of an artificial lake nestled in a woods. At one extremity is a symmetrical concrete abutment, the massive pasty appearance of which is markedly out of keeping with the nearby stand of hemlock and hard woods, but at the other extremity is a fishing bay as beautiful as any an angler ever beheld. There is a stump-strewn surface with small beds of lily pads here and there, mossy ledges outcropping on a steep bank, and low-hanging foliage shading water four feet in depth. The stream, which has been dammed, cascades down the valley out of the west. The impounding of its silt-free water has transformed transparency into azure blue. To me, this man-made lake is better than nature's own, just because of the stumps.

The largemouth bass of Enchanted Pond, and I call it that though it is not its name, are well fed and highly colored. When they cruise in the water or jump into the air, a broad lateral line of the darkest green is predominant. The spot casting beside the stumps, in the openings among the pads, and under the overhanging branches by the shore line is target fishing at its best. The incidents that rush toward recollection are interesting, but they are secondary to the recollection of their setting.

As schoolboys of tender years, we first learn of exceptions when the complicated matter of the number of days in each month is presented in catchy rhyme. Then the spelling teacher confounds us with an involved set of inconsistencies to a series of rules. Later, Latin class introduces its declensions, irregular verbs, and i-stems. By the time we have arrived at the age of fifteen, exception is such a thoroughly established part of education that we begin to look for it in other places, and it appears everywhere. The word *exceptional* becomes a favorite, and we are of the honest belief that it is the exception that proves the rule. The effect of fishing on the state of the mind is described as follows by Washington Irving: "There is certainly something in angling that tends to produce a gentleness of spirit and a serenity of mind." To confirm the accuracy of this precept of the Chronicler of Tarrytown, we point to the only exception of whom we have knowledge, the galvanic Oliver Seipe. Once at the waterside he is excitable, impatient, and reckless. There is nothing tranquil about his mental state, his actions, or his appearance.

Like a horse chafing at the bit, he is under the spell of a do-or-die, let-'er-rip attitude. Falling in, tearing waders, breaking rods, snagging hooks, and—worst of all to him—losing large fish are all a part of his day outdoors. He could find big bass, he could hook big bass, but he could not land a big bass. That is, he could not accomplish this feat for a long time.

The day of recompense finally arrived at the spot that is a veritable graveyard for lures, to which "What Price" Oliver had contributed a noble share. After the last jump of the fish, after the last lunge, and after the final wild sweep of the net, which happened to engulf the bass, Oliver admired his highly prized and deep appreciated trophy. He blinked his eyes and pinched himself—no, it was not a dream this time. Back at the restaurant he would produce the goods and would act nonchalant about the showing of the fish, just as most of the other fellows usually do.

He was standing on a peculiar green island, peculiar in that it was a clump of aquatic vegetation, with some six inches of water flowing among the green stems, appearing to be a solid green bank above the surface. The prize was slipped into a live bag, and the drawstring was anchored by a long stick that was sunk deeply into the rocks and gravel.

After fishing for about fifteen minutes, he returned to the spot to admire the bass. There it was, but it was not in the bag. It had pushed its way out of the opening and was resting among the weeds, back protruding above the surface, two feet in front of the bag.

Heart in mouth, Oliver crouched, worked his way in closer, then made a dive-landing with his digestive organs flush on top of his fish. The splash was great and the coverage complete. Long legs kicked as long arms clawed. It was a tense moment; then he realized he had achieved success, for that jagging sensation in his stomach was caused by the dorsal fin of the fish. No defensive football player ever nailed a fast, elusive halfback with greater dispatch. Sputtering and splashing, bruised and pricked, as wet as Niagara, and glasses covered with beads of water, he struggled blindly to his feet, but the only thing that mattered was that slimy, wiggling fish held in a grip like that of death.

Homemade Lures

Drawings by George Meyerreicks

The caster knows no joy greater than the successful design and fabrication of a highly effective lure. This is saying a great deal because catching an exceptional fish is a tremendous experience, and there is abundant satisfaction in knowing that one has enjoyed a successful excursion and has fished the water well.

Lures are tools of angling. The tools the angler needs to produce the lures can be simple and few in number or they can be elaborate and numerous. Lloyd King, "the Juniata King," a famous Pennsylvania bass fisherman who is gone now, made his pet lures with a penknife. However, Bob Bates, a mutual friend of Lloyd's and mine, had a spindle machine (a treacherous contraption), a hard-to-secure jeweler's lathe, a combination thirty-five pound air compressor and air brush, along with a special cloth for scale-finish painting, electric drills with all appendages, and just about every other type of lure-making implement and apparatus. The point is, you can tool up to suit your fancy in order to produce your own lures.

Over the years I was involved with two teams that were

honestly attempting to create something special, something better than anything commercially available, in order to meet specific angling requirements. We were not making lures just for the sake of lure making. There was always a specific goal. It is not the purpose of this chapter merely to describe how to make lures at home. Rather it is my hope that the following directions for making certain unobtainable great lures will make it possible for them to be placed in appreciative hands.

Apothecary's weight is the system the manufacturers employ. A balance scale measures weight in grains and ounces. In this system of measurement there are 480 grains to the ounce, which divides up thus: ¼ ounce—120 grains; ⅜ ounce—180; ½ ounce—240; ⅝ ounce—300; ¾ ounce—360. Each coat of paint on a ¼- to ⅜-ounce lure weighs approximately twenty grains.

There is no reason to tolerate in a casting lure either a lack of pulling power or excessive air resistance. Pulling power results from a combination of sufficient weight and acceptable aerodynamics.

One thing we cannot discount is the trial-and-error experimentation and the intense interest displayed by the early lure makers. They patterned their procedures after those of the exacting gunsmiths and the reel makers, many of whom were watchmakers. These pioneers included such casters as Jim Heddon, Ans Decker, J. K. Rush, Bill Jamison, Al Foss, Ivar Hennings, and Robert McGarrough. They were perfectionists to whom time, care, and craftsmanship were taken for granted and were not considered cost factors, as is the case today. Some of these great old lures, now all but lost in the dust of time, can have new life breathed into them by the lure-making hobbyist. The home lure maker can also produce new conceptions of his own.

None of the seven following lures, the directions for fabricating which are outlined, are currently available, but all are tremendous for their respective uses. Any caster would do well to test their attractions.

Size: 1″-1¼″
¼ oz-½ oz
Hook: 4/0
Finishes: yellow
  yellow, black and white
See back endleaf.

Mack's Minno-Bug

The first of my special favorites falls into the weighted-fly-and-spinner category. My personal rating of it is that no finer lure for bigmouths of the lakes has ever been produced. I am sold on it, you see, and think of it as something beloved. Even if the master craftsman who created and produced it had not lost his life in a tragic canoe accident, it is doubtful whether the lure, great as it is, could have withstood the ravages of the low-unit-cost era in which metal baits are cranked out like sausages.

When we could no longer replenish our supplies from the inventory at McGarrough's San Antonio ranch, we tried to make our own. The first ones we turned out were sick excuses, but we persevered.

Examine the picture of the bare body. This is a ⅜-ounce McGarrough Minno-Bug from which the hair and feathers have been stripped. The little metal loop is for the attachment of a strip of pork rind, should that be desired, and it should be considered optional.

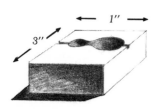

The compact metal body, with its sloping underside and flat top, into which the single hook is molded, is basic to the lure. In order to make the body, one must first make a mold into which the hook is placed before the molten lead is poured.

The first job is to make the mold. Steel would be ideal, but not being a tool-and-die man, I turned to baked clay and also to hardwood. A depression in the shape of the Minno-Bug body must be formed in a rectangular block.

Before inserting the hook into the mold, the shank of the hook should be wrapped lightly with thread in order that the metal will adhere to it and hold the hook firmly. This is important.

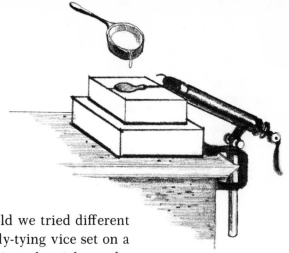

To set the hook exactly right in the mold we tried different devices, the best of which seemed to be a fly-tying vice set on a lower plane, to hold the hook point up at just the right angle, preparatory to pouring in the molten lead.

Old linotype is practically the same as plain lead. It should be melted in a small iron receptacle with a handle, like a miniature frying pan.

The body is painted by hand. The big, fancy bug eyes make it more attractive, at least to people if not to fish.

The hook and body now being one, it is time to tie in the bucktail and two streamers. The tier of the minnow-type hair trout fly will understand this operation. The hook is secured in a fly-tying vice, point down, and the hair is tied in chunk by chunk. The normal thing would be to use heavy thread (nylon) in a bobbin, but McGarrough used fine, fairly soft wire. If desired, hairs of different colors can be used on the same bug. The streamer-fly feathers, or maribou, mylar, or ostrich or peacock herl, is then added. Every fly tier will understand how this is done. The excess hair toward the eye is trimmed with a scissors, creating a neat stubble collar around the neck of the lure.

The final step is to attach to the eye of the hook the best-looking June Bug spinner you have been able to locate, size 2/0, or larger if you prefer. *(See photo above left.)*

What a bass lure this makes! My vote goes to yellow or yellow and black, but in the days of Mack McGarrough I saw many largemouths, and smallmouths too, caught on just about every one of his twelve beautiful patterns, each with a catchy name, such as, Widow, Black Prince, Mack's Favorite, Yellow Sally, Light Buck, and Queen.

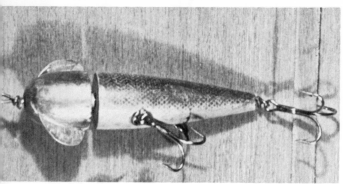

Size: 2″-4″
Hook: #6-2/0
Finish: Bass: yellow
* Muskie: metallic green and copper*
See front endleaf.

Whirligig

When it comes to lures, you will find that Fox is dogmatic. To me, the Whirligig is the greatest of all lures for fishing for bass and muskies or bass and northern pike at the same time. This is a skim-and-swim lure, and it is complicated.

Work down a piece of red cedar or poplar on a lathe so that it has a fat head and a taper graduated to a thin tail. It should have an overall length of three to four inches.

Either drill or have a woodworker drill a hole lengthwise through the center of the lure, the diameter of the hole being 1/32 of an inch. To do it right, a jig to hold the blank should be constructed.

Next the head is sawed off vertically about ¾ of an inch from the tip of the nose.

Several things must be done to the head before the lure is assembled. With a hacksaw, cut two diagonal slots on opposite sides of the head almost to the drilled center hole. These slots will accommodate the small metal wings or ears, which are cut with shears from aluminum. The metal can be shaped with a file before being inserted in the slot. A piece of brass or aluminum tubing 1/32 of an inch in diameter, the length of the head only, is placed in the drilled part.

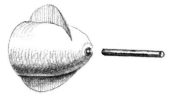

It is best, though not necessary, if a depression is drilled in the body where the screw eye carrying the belly hook is to be located. It is better, too, if the hole for the screw eye is pre-drilled before the head and body are joined to prevent splitting.

The next step is to fashion the shaft, which has a loop on the front end and is twisted to hold a treble hook on the tail. A carefully straightened large-size Gem ''General'' paper clip is ideal.

A loop is made in one end of the straightened paper clip and a little washer-disc with convex side toward loop is placed on the clip. The shaft now goes through the tubing of the head. Another concave/convex washer-disc is now placed on the shaft, facing in same direction as the first.

The shaft is run through the body of the blank. With a sharp-nose pliers start a loop in the shaft at the tail, slip on the treble hook, and finish the loop. Now screw on the belly hook.

One word of warning: If that head is not free to spin under the slightest pressure, the entire lure will twist. On small models—lures that weigh less than ⅜ of an ounce—it is usually necessary to wrap a few turns of lead wire around the shaft of the belly screw eye before it is screwed into place, so as to prevent the entire lure from turning and twisting the line.

Size: 2"
¼ oz
Hook: #4
Finish: Bass: yellow/day
black/night
brown
See front endleaf.

Baby Popper

There is no warning when a lure ceases to be manufactured. It just fades out of the market. I was caught short by the discontinuation of the Rush Tango Minnow, Heddon's Game Fisher, Al Foss's Shimmy Wiggler, Mack's Minno-Bug, and the Shakespeare Midget Spinner, but not by the passing of the Shakespeare Baby Popper. Salted away was a box full of assorted patterns, and there were still others in my working assortment.

As the name indicates, the Baby Popper is a surface lure, but one possessing a unique action. Up front is an oversize concave face. In back there is a trim tail, which furnishes just enough support for the back treble hook. The result is that at rest the lure floats in a vertical position, and slight twitches of the rod tip bring it level, so that the big face catches water, sometimes leaving a bubble as big as a tennis ball, which promptly explodes.

If memory serves me correctly, this short-lived lure made its appearance in the early 1940s, before spinning and spin casting were popularized in this country. If it was not the tiniest lure on the market at that time, it was surely one of the smallest, weighing in at a very slight ¼-ounce. There was a good reason for this. Only in its diminutive size was the lure light enough for the tail hook to pull it into the vertical position at rest.

The body of the lure is turned on a lathe. The important thing is to keep it small and to thin down the tail.

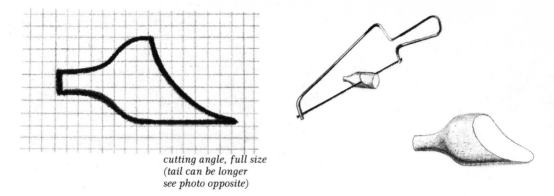

*cutting angle, full size
(tail can be longer
see photo opposite)*

It may be necessary to turn to a woodworker to saw out the face, the alternative being a jigsaw or a sabre saw.

wrong

right

Once the hardware is attached—this includes the screw eye in the face and the belly and tail screw eyes and hooks—the lure should be put in the water to see if it tips into the necessary vertical position when at rest. If it simply lies level, more weight is needed at the tail. A thicker and longer screw eye and a heavy salt-water hook on the tail may do the trick. If this is not sufficient, several turns of wire lead around the neck of the tail screw eye should create the desired result.

Once the lure is painted, there is the possibility of an attractive addition. A rubber skirt can be placed around the midsection of the lure in such a way that it floats away from the tail at rest and lies back during the cast, offering little additional air resistance.

It is more satisfactory to purchase rubber skirts than to attempt to cut them out of a piece of colored rubber with scissors. The commercial ones can be opened up, that is removed from the small tube, then spread out and wrapped around the body of the Baby Popper and sealed in place with Epoxy glue.

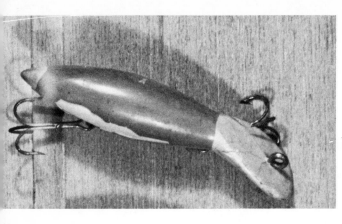

Size: 4''-5''
½oz-¾oz
Hook: 4/0-2/0
Finish: Bass: yellow and red
*   Muskie: metallic green and hot copper*
See back endleaf.

Rush Tango Minnow

For several seasons my favorite lure for pike and bass in the Blue Sea Lake area of Quebec was a floating underwater wobbler called the Rush Tango Minnow. It not only had an erratic swimming action of considerable attraction but it also dug down deeper than the Pikie Minnows, Vamps, and Bass Orenos.

Suddenly my supply was down to two Baby Rush Tangos and one beaten-up, badly scarred regular one, and the stores no longer carried them. The creator was gone and so were his lures.

Research shed some light on the history of this superb lure. Its maker was J. K. Rush of Syracuse, N.Y. It was advertised in the May, 1921, issue of *National Sportsman* (under the sketch herewith reproduced) as follows: "The Rush Tango Minnow is the original swimming, diving wobbler bait."

This sheds some light on the early history of plugs. We know this one predated the year 1917. It must have been placed on the market before Ivar Hennings developed and sold the Bass Oreno, which marked the start of the South Bend Bait Company.

The Rush Tango Minnow has great pulling power and castability, two qualities that present-day manufacturers are inclined to overlook. The big, flat lip and the thick, solid body combine to produce one of the all-time greats among bass, pike, and muskie plugs.

An appeal of this plug to the hobbyist lure maker is the fact that the blank can easily be worked down on a lathe. A saw then takes care of the wooden lip.

Red cedar is my favorite wood for plugs, but poplar is excellent and walnut a possibility. Keep away from soft woods such as white pine and balsa, they do not provide pulling power and are unsafe for screw eyes. And keep alway also from the hardest woods, such as locust or hickory, because they do not float properly and are difficult to work.

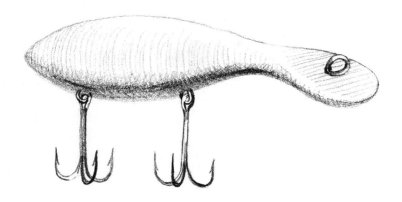

As in all wooden lures, holes should be drilled for screw eyes and oil placed on the threads before the fittings are screwed into place, lest the heads be twisted off as the screws are inserted.

Size: 4''-5''
½oz-¾oz
Hook: # 4-4/0
Finish: Natural wood
. . .other injured minnows:
     scale finish / day
     black / night
See front endleaf.

The Pocono Cedar Plug

It appears that J. L. Boorse was the first to make and use this injured-minnow-type surface plug. He fished it with great success on stream smallmouths and pond bigmouths and chain pickerel. It was later manufactured in Allentown and Easton, Pennsylvania, the latter being the home town of Samuel Phillippi, who made the first split, glued, and wrapped bamboo rods.

Mr. Boorse, who now resides along Skippack Creek in Montgomery County, Pennsylvania, presented me with several of his beautiful lures with the sensitive propellers, which were made after he lost his eyesight. There was a time when he did fine work on guns. Today he fabricates beautiful and elaborate coffee tables.

His Cedar Plug is primarily a cripple-minnow type, but it is unique in two respects. The body material is red cedar, and sometimes when the blank is worked on a lathe, a two-tone effect results. Red cedar is well known for irregular waves of dark wood beside waves of white wood. The function of the heavier dark wood is structural, whereas the white wood carries the sap up and down the trunk and branches. The second feature is the extremely sensitive fore-and-aft propellers with opposite twists, which Mr. Boorse dies out of soft aluminum, drills through for shafts, then bends to shape. Instead of running a shaft completely through the body of the blank, he makes a neat loop on the end of each of two pieces of nonspringy wire about one and a half inches in length and drills appropriate holes in the body of the lure. Then, after assembling the propellers and ring washers, he sets the two wires into the body with Epoxy glue.

Another style of propeller

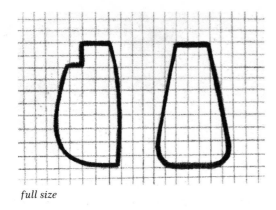

full size

Size: 1¼″
¼oz
Hook: #4
Finish: frog finish
(green and yellow)
See back endleaf.

Pad Jumper

Bob Bates and I wanted a dual-purpose lure that would be better than anything available, so we set out to make it. It was to be fished in pad fields, so it was named before it was designed. It was also to be used for hazard fishing across algae islands and in streamside brush piles. This turned out to be quite an enterprise, for an effective model was as elusive as the will-o-the-wisp. Finally Bob did it.

back is tapered

front is wide

The top of the head is flat, the front is wide, the belly is carefully rounded, and the back is tapered. When this lure lands on its back, it rolls over as though it were alive.

belly is rounded

The original double hook, hook points up, was fairly weedless. Then I got an idea for an one-hundred-percent weedless plug. Attached on the back was a single hook, with the point up. This hook point is run down the nose of a plastic worm and brought out the neck. It is then turned halfway around and the point over the barb is put back in the worm. This is the same principle utilized by the professional tournament fishermen. The answering strike of the angler must have authority.

top of head is flat

Size: 1½"-3
Hook: # 4
Finish: varied
See front endleaf.

Spark Plug

EDITOR'S NOTE: When this book was written, these two lures were available on the market. The Penn-Dart Company failed, and now, by necessity, these lures must be homemade.

Work down a piece of red cedar or poplar on a lathe so that it is tapered from head to tail, the thinest point being at the head and the thickest part ¾ of the way back to the tapered stub tail.

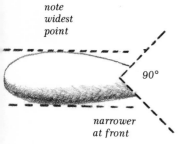

note
widest
point

90°

narrower
at front

When the body of the lure is still turning in the lathe, smooth it with fine sandpaper or emery cloth. After removal from the lathe, surround the blank with corrugated cardboard for protection, then place it firmly in a vice in a vertical position, head-up. The mouth, a perfect right angle, is cut away with a hack saw in such a manner that the lower lip is slightly longer than the upper lip.

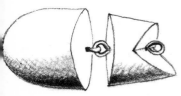

A centered hole in the apex of the mouth is drilled for the screweye, which is then snuggly inserted in the open face.

Spark plug can be made up as a jointed lure and in such form it is a shallow underwater swimmer posessing violent action. After the lure is sawed into two pieces, the back part being slightly longer than the fore section, wood must be filed away from the sides of each portion to provide wiggling room. Interlocked screweyes, one in a horizontal position, one in a vertical position, are placed in predrilled holes.

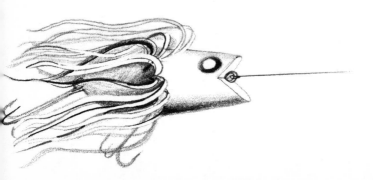

Size:: 3''-7''
Hook: # 6-2/0
Finish: varied
See back endleaf.

Sick sucker floats at rest; under rod-tip manipulation it bobs, weaves and angles on the surface; and it is a side-to-side under-water swimmer when reeled rapidly. The blank is worked down on a lathe from a fairly blunt nose to a gently tapered thin tail.

Place it in water to determine the proper location of the back and the belly. From the underside, ¾ of an inch from the nose, saw a vertical cut almost half through. Then from just under the nose saw a horizontal cut, which is at right angle to first.

In order to shape the lower lip into a V with point toward the nose, mark with a pencil the points where the sawing should follow. This is done on each side. The wood is then cut away with a knife. It can be trimmed and shaped to appear to be smiling.

To make a neat job the roof of the mouth and the lips can be evened up with a flat saw. Holes are drilled where the screweyes are to be placed. The lure can be equipped with two or three treble hooks as desired.

Sick Sucker

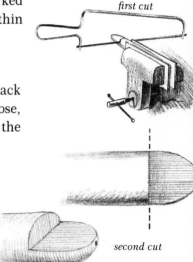

first cut

second cut

third cut

fourth cut

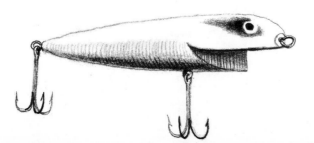

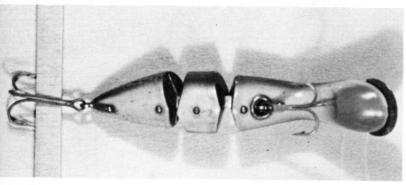

Size: 4"-5"
½oz-¾oz
Hook:4/0-2/0
Finish: Bass: yellow and orange
 Muskie: green scale
See back endleaf.

Game Fisher

A tremendous lure of the 1920s was Heddon's Game Fisher, the first jointed plug. Ross Riddle, a manufacturer's rep, once told me that he considered it the greatest of all lures for muskies in the Lake of the Woods region of Ontario. This one cannot be worked on a lathe. Considerable hand work is entailed. There is a regular and a baby version of this lure, the former having two joints and three pieces, the latter one joint and two pieces.

Prepare a wood blank as shown on page 227. After it has been worked into shape with a wood rasp to conform with the silhouette shown in the illustration, the piece is cut into two or three sections. The next operation is to cut away extra wood, making possible a wiggle at the hinges.

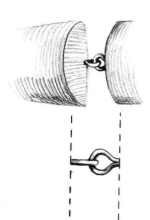

The Heddon craftsmen did an elaborate job of hinging the sections. Metal strips were inserted in slots in the wood and held together by pins. (See photo above.) But there is a more simple way to accomplish the hinging. A hinged connection utilizing screw eyes at the midpoints between sections is quite satisfactory. One screw eye is placed in a vertical position, and the other is placed horizontally, the two being interlocked.

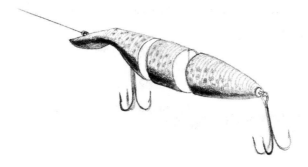

Finishes

Finish may be more important to the angler than to the bass, but no one can be condemned for doing a superior painting job. The following instructions will enable one to obtain the ultimate in finishes on wooden lures.

After working down the blank on a lathe, smooth the wood with sandpaper while still turning the blank in the lathe. Follow this with a further smoothing with emery cloth.

After a mouth or face is made with a hacksaw, it can be smoothed and polished with a flat-sided fine-tooth file.

Put on a base coat of white paint made specially for that purpose, then sand smooth by hand. Repeat this same procedure and you are ready for a coat of the basic color. Good wood paints are available, Tessar's products being the ones with which I happen to be familiar.

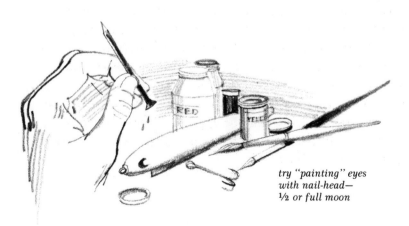

try "painting" eyes with nail-head— ½ or full moon

A special favorite of mine is an odd concoction. From an art shop I secure small containers of Venus granulated metallic coloring. Among other colors, it comes in green, gold, and hot copper. I like to add some gold to both the green and the copper to brighten them. This material is added to Tessar's Dope (or any other clear lacquer) and painted on the lure.

Scale finishes can be done in an elaborate manner calling for specialized equipment or they can be achieved simply and cheaply. The first requisite is cloth with round holes in the weave, which I suppose might be called curtain cloth. Among other supplies, this can be secured from fly-tying and lure-making equipment houses, such as Herter's in Waseca, Minnesota, and Hille's in Williamsport, Pennsylvania. These suppliers are also good sources of hooks, screw eyes, ring-washers, beads, wire shafts, metal lips, propellers, and other lure-making materials.

The professionals at the plants use an air compressor and a spray brush, the kind employed in commercial art work. A convenient holder for the cloth is the old-type, round, metal holder used for embroidery work. The lure is held directly on one side of the cloth. The spray apparatus is held several inches back on the other side. One color scale can be put on top of another to create unusual and beautiful effects. Vertical stripes, like those of a tiger muskie, can be applied on top of other scale finishes. The scale finishes can be made to taper into a solid colored stripe on the back.

Stencils can be cut and used.

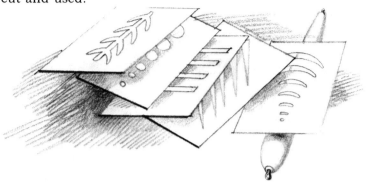

The only equipment of this nature that I have used was a thirty-five-pound air compressor with a light motor and a pen-shaped instrument with a reservoir on the side. It was necessary to work fast with this so the "brush" would not clog with drying paint, and it had to be thoroughly washed when a change of color was in order.

The cheap way—and it looks good—is something else again. After the basic color has dried, the lure is wrapped in one layer of the curtain cloth. This can be held in place with clothesline clips. Wear a good-for-nothing jacket or shirt and glove. Hold the lure away from the body at arm's length. With the other hand give the side of the lure a good spray from a can of compressed paint. Turn the lure around and give it a spraying on the opposite side. An application of a second color of scale finish is an added attraction. The glove and jacket will be ruined.

A wonderful outer finish that is practically indestructible is made by smearing on a layer of Epoxy glue.

Conclusion

My mood is one of delight as I sit along a friendly bank of Possum Lake, reveling in the pleasure of looking for signs of muskies on the prowl and starting the final chapter of *The Book of Lures*. A pencil and pad are in hand, and propped nearby against a bush is my casting outfit, ready to go. To me, outdoor writing has always been in equal proportions both a pleasure and a business. The major hobby is angling, the minor hobby is writing about it.

In retrospect I realize how wonderful it was for me to have lived when I did. The greatest time ever for the outdoor man was during the years directly after World War I. Luck dictated that I grow up with the development and popularization of lure fishing in America as well as the advancement of American dry-fly fishing for trout, and in both I played a part. Our fishing forefathers never knew equipment then such has since become commonplace and easily available to us. Those were also the halcyon days of grouse hunting, when the birds flushed in groups, and there were bucks with rocking-chair racks in the mountains, which were covered with immature second growth.

At first hunting and fishing pressure was light, but it was

destined to multiply tremendously under the combination of a growing population, easily available transportation, increased free time, and intense promotion. Time changes all things, and all things are relative. It is because of this relativity that it is as good to get out fishing today as it was yesterday, and it will be just as good tomorrow.

I look now across the bay to the shady depths and see an angler silhouetted against the green. It is wonderful out here. The nonanglers can never understand what they have missed. Fishing itself is far from being all there is to it. There is the caress of the breeze, the song of the birds, the gamut of greens in foliage, the noise of murmuring waters, the billowing clouds under a blue heaven. I need things like these, and I know that because you are an angler the same feelings are manifest in you. We are in rapport with Nature.

An historical summary is in order:

"Plugging!" That magic exclamation suggests big fish. Bass and muskies are the chief targets, but other game fish hit the wares of the caster in varying degrees. This phase of angling, as American as baseball and ice-cream cones, is the only type of fishing developed exclusively in this country.

Kentucky watchmakers produced the first quadruple multiplying reels. Great rod builders perfected suitable sticks for the delivery of the goods. Advanced manufacturing methods produced suitable lines. For some decades the new sport, which captivated the fancy of thousands, was devoted to the casting of live bait. Appropriately enough it was called bait casting.

Someone then made the discovery that bass could be more easily attracted than deceived. The "plug" was established. Because of the convenience and effectiveness of this lure, a new game caught fire and spread, but the old nomenclature held firm. Bait casting it was, and bait casting it shall be, even though live bait has passed out of the picture. Casting lures, however, are sometimes referred to as "baits." When deceivers gave way to attractors, ingenuity was given a free rein and imagination ran rampant. Plugs made their commercial bow.

Design after design, cloaked in many colors and with one kind of action after another, quickly made their appearance.

This ushered in a new fishing era. Traditionally, anyone who chose to fish went fishin', and he could go pretty much where he pleased and could keep as many fish as he could catch. The first generation of plug fisherman was numbered in the thousands. Two decades later their number totaled more than a million.

The increased fishing pressure in the new age of mobility was sure to have consequences, both for the fish and the fisherman. On the one hand, fish became increasingly shy and fewer in numbers and therefore more difficult to catch. On the other, man was led to provide some protection for his quarry by instigating game laws. Gone were the days when the "Kalamazoo-style" caster crashed his "dowjak" over a nest to provoke the charge of the guardian bass. The confident, inquisitive fish of yesteryear have long since ended up on a stringer. Their successors are wiser but fewer in number. Gone, too, are the days when only a handful fished any given body of water.

As times changed, the thinking of the fishermen changed with them. Analysis and resourcefulness were applied. The smart fishermen recognized that the new situation must be met with refinement. They altered their tackle and changed their approaches. Others observing their superior results followed suit. Light lures appeared on the market along with balanced tackle—longer rods, more delicate reels, and lighter lines—that was specifically designed to handle them. Two types of fixed-spool reels, spinning and spin-casting types, made their appearance. Lure casting was developing into a subtle game.

As with all sports, it became evident that here was a percentage proposition, and it pays to play percentages. A pattern gradually took shape. Target fishing with deadly accuracy and long casts became the order of the day, and along with it came control in answering the strike of the fish, so that the hooks could be driven home, and control in fighting the fish, so as to minimize the difficulties presented by hazards.

Forethought and trial-and-error established procedures. A surface lure was found to be in a class of its own in the evening and at night, and it was discovered that it should usually be fished slowly in the shallows. The sinking propeller plug was seen to be particularly effective in flowing water, but it also turned out to be great in lakes when the surface was broken by raindrops. Largemouths loved the weighted bucktail-and-spinner combination, whereas the pike family preferred the flash of a spoon. Walleyes were susceptible to a slow-going, deep-running sinking wabbler retrieved at the level of the school. Hot-weather daytime lake fishing for smallmouths was a matter of combing the depths of shaded water, but these same fish could be found in the shallows at night. Some fished the floating wabbler on the surface, then retrieved it underwater, using the skim-and-swim technique.

Any big fish, and particularly a large old bass, has one marked weakness in an otherwise strong sales resistance to man's attractors. The flat smack of a small lure diving into the water in a lifelike manner is frequently met with a spontaneous reaction. The big fellow does not stop to look and think. He turns viciously on the lure, seizing it crosswise. The smaller fish are more prone to strike during the course of the retrieve.

There is a little casting trick that pays royal dividends and places an angler head and shoulders above the average. The lure is cast in a low arc, and just before it enters the water the rod tip is lifted as the line is checked. This starts the lure on its way back toward the angler, resulting in the highly desirable and lifelike silent dive cast.

There was a time when plugging could not be learned quickly, simply because the necessary educated thumb comes by way of long practice. But now there is a royal road. An experience of my wife's will illustrate the point. She could handle a fly rod, but she knew nothing of bait casting. The first day we spent together plugging for smallmouths on the beautiful Susquehanna River she had a miserable time of it picking out the inevitable bird's nests. The next day she tried again, but this time with a Johnson push-button reel equipped with the line that comes on it, instead of the fast and touchy quadruple multiplier. Her problem was solved; casts were satisfactory, and she enjoyed the outing.

Those who cherish lure casting are wed to their short rods with backbone, efficient reels and lines, and wonderful lures. They have always thought highly of bass, and now they like muskies too. These guys and gals will keep plugging away, only to be followed by generations from the same mold, many of whom will be fishing in waters that did not even exist in Dad's day.

Appendix

A Short History of Conservation

The voice in the wilderness was that of the angler. "Pure water is basic," it cried. "All life is contingent upon it." But it was the age of materialism, the era of the concept that water was free—to do with as anyone chooses. Society had settled on the idea that nature existed to be exploited by man.

The angler was alone. Others knew him to be a hobbyist; therefore, they reasoned, he has an axe to grind. All he is interested in is a few little fish; what he has to say about the quality of water as it affects health and life is an excuse, not an important concern.

In the 1880s the angler was joined in the campaign to conserve natural resources by the hunter and the forester. So it was that the protective philosophy was given a broader base.

A clear conception of the situation as it then existed is necessary to see the significance of a certain event in its full context. The first period of environmental deterioration was interrupted by the Civil War. Then a two-headed monster waxed fat on exploitation as it crossed mountains and plains. One head gorged itself on the vegetation while the other gobbled up the creatures of nature. Part of the trail was ashen gray, part the brown of erosion, and part blood red.

In the wake of the axe there was left a tinder box, a forest floor littered with dry limbs. The most valuable wood was white pine—straight-grained, free of knots, easily worked, and exceedingly valuable for building purposes. Although the wood from hemlock was not as good, being brittle and coarse-grained, its thick bark was rich in tannic acid, exactly what was needed at the tanneries. Often when a prostrate hemlock was stripped of its bark, the trunk was left to rot.

Primeval forest stands of these two conifers were so dense that every square rod yielded one or more trees. Trunks grew straight and tall, bare of branches almost to the top. Some single trees furnished five logs of sixteen feet in length and from twenty to forty inches in diameter. This was the form in which they were floated down the watersheds to the mill towns.

A second lumbering wave concentrated on the scattered hardwoods. This forest product was used in the manufacture of furniture and farm implements, for the construction of vehicles, and for railroad ties and mine props. If an immature tree would yield so much as one railroad tie, down it came. The pine logs were floated from the woods to the mills, but in the case of the deciduous trees, the mills came to the woods.

The plowman mined his rectangular plots for their fertility, knowing that when they were played out, there was always virgin soil for the taking to the west. When the range was overgrazed, the cattleman could establish new herds on the grass lands in the direction of the setting sun.

So, the population shifted with the plucking of the fruits of the land. America was on the move—westward. Wealth beckoned beyond. At first, the way West was negotiated in the "prairie schooner," the sturdy wagon made at the jump-off point along the Conestoga River in Penn's Woods. With it went an amazing shooting iron, also fabricated in Lancaster County, an accurate muzzle-loading rifle that had its barrel bored with lands and groves to make the bullet spin, thus giving it great accuracy and distance. This was the long-range game-getter that made it possible to live off the land. Sam Colt's pistol with the revolving cylinder served a more personal use.

Finally there was woven westward a network of steel to speed the movement. Young men went West as the Great Northern Railway offered, "greatly reduced Colonist rates" —one-way tickets.

Such a ready market for meat and hides developed that commercial hunting was a prosperous business. Under this pressure great herds disappeared like snow in springtime, until there was nothing but the dregs in the bottom of the wildlife barrel. Life was soon to pass from the last heath hen, and the passenger pigeon would fly no more. Buffalo, antelope, deer, and other creatures were at their nadir. So were trout in the rivers, except in the coastal streams of the Pacific.

Raging forest fires persisted. When the ashes were washed away, the mountain often showed its bare bones. The good earth lost its ability to absorb rainfall and then slowly deliver it to the underground water channels from which it could out-crop at the springs. No longer could the ground hold the water like a sponge for a time of need. Instead, the water rushed down the bleak hills into the streams and carried with it, in the form of silt, the finest top soil. In some spots nothing but rock remained upon which no living thing was ever again to grow. Fire, which scarred the fertility from the soil, continued to follow the lumberjack and the bull wacker. Washed gullies appeared. Floods became more devastating, droughts were more acute. The great blotter had been set back a millennium.

It was early in the year 1883 that a young man, a bespectacled little fellow, rode the iron horse into the Bad Lands of North Dakota, where he intended to spend his time in hunting and "roughing it." All that he knew about the West came from reading, but he was familiar with the changing watersheds of his native New York.

Although the trip was enjoyable and successful, he did not like what he saw. Everyone regarded game as a commercial resource, whereas he looked upon it as a recreational resource.

It was obvious to young Teddy Roosevelt that without control and protection, buffalo herds, bands of antelope, and other resources were facing the twilight zone. It was just a question of time until the great forests of the Pacific Northwest would go the way of those of the middle-Atlantic states and New England, with the resultant deterioration of the streams. Too many people were either ignorant or selfish.

Twenty-four-year-old Roosevelt returned home a dedicated man—and the owner of a North Dakota ranch. He would do all in his power to preserve the American heritage he cherished. Help was needed and there would have to be organization, so his initial move was to band together kindred spirits, including men of influence, in what he named the Boone and Crockett Club. So it was that at precisely the time when leadership was so desperately needed, a self-appointed leader, a farsighted and vocal one, took charge.

New York benefited first, for he soon became the Governor of the Empire State. In due time, as President of the United States, he took his campaign to all the people. His inaugural message, delivered December 2, 1901, expressed the following fundamental ideas—forestry is the perpetuation of the forest by use, with controlled cutting to protect watersheds; there must be government-owned areas with wildlife refuges therein; market hunting must cease; preservation must became a part of state government. Thus the first conservation movement was launched.

Then a Pennsylvania forester—and skilled angler—became a part of the Federal Administration. The influence on and assistance to President Roosevelt of Gifford Pinchot was great, and each in turn utilized his power to the utmost. Pinchot founded the Society of American Foresters.

At this time there was no word or term to describe the inter-relationship of waters, soils, forests, fish, and game—all of the natural resources. In his autobiography, *Breaking New Ground*, Pinchot told how he had discussed the matter with Overton Price, an associate in the Forest Service, and from this had come the word "conservation." He did not recall which one conceived the term, but there is no question about the identity of the individual who put it in the dictionary. The President liked it to such a degree that conservation became the keynote of his administration.

Conservationist Tama Jim Wilson, in paraphrasing Thoreau, sounded the principle, now often quoted: "The question will always be decided from the standpoint of the greatest good for the greatest number in the long run."

Will Dilge, one of the great fishermen of the land, saw some of the waters he fished poisoned by the tanneries, other streams converted into useless acid-soaked water from coal washings and mine drainage, and still others turned into running sores by sewage and industrial wastes. Deeply concerned, he met with some of his angling cronies and the outcome of the gathering was the formation of the Izaak Walton League of America, "defender of soil, water and wildlife." So it was that the angler and the hunter officially banded together in local groups to form a national organization that became both a rallying point and a mouthpiece for conservationists.

Members soon understood that the people and their government encouraged the development and exploitation of natural resources; to them degradation of water quality was an irrelevant sort of thing. Of minimum concern was a place where fish could live and where swimming was safe. The influence of Teddy Roosevelt had eroded after his death as the population and industrial growth increased.

The Darwinian notion that the human race is a part of nature could not gain public acceptance. To pollute was socially and economically acceptable conduct because it saved money for cities and increased corporate profits. The primeval atmosphere was no longer intact and deterioration intensified. A growing list of extinct species came into being, plus a list of eighty-nine birds and mammals threatened by extermination.

Once the hunters and fishermen were well-organized, interest spread and knowledge grew. Member "Ikes" learned from each other, from officials of conservation departments, and from the technical papers of the Wildlife Management Institute and the Sport Fishing Institute. A general understanding took form.

In the second quarter of the twentieth century the first Pure Streams Law was enacted as a public-health measure. The writer was a young man then, and by quirk of circumstances the son of the judge who heard the first pollution case listed in the courts of Pennsylvania, and, to the best of our knowledge, in the country. No matter what the verdict, appeal was a certainty, and the opinion would be precedent-setting. My father received a heavy amount of mail before the trial, and most of the writers were laboring under the misconception that it was the role of the court to pass judgment on the merits and demerits of the Act. At least seventy-five percent of the correspondents spoke as fishermen.

The polluter was found guilty of breaking the new law and ordered to cease and desist. Ultimately the decision of the lower court was upheld by the State Supreme Court and the precedent was set for future water-pollution cases.

The 50s and 60s marked new and vital threats. Almost overnight, traditional freedoms, involving every individual and every social and economic interest, were far out of balance. The elements upon which life hinges, the air, the water, and the land, were subject to pollution. Man was badly out of tune with the heartbeat of the earth.

Pesticides were changing the ecology, and the first to see it were the outdoor people. Then weed killer and chemical fertilizers turned upon man. Violent fish kills took place in what heretofore had been water quite suitable for aquatic life.

The medical profession made known a horrible set of facts. DDT, which kills by attacking the nervous system, collects in the bones and tissues of the organisms that eat it—but it is stored indirectly and in greater quantity in the creatures that devour the original consumer. It is even transferred to a child through the milk which is consumed. DDT remains in the land ten years or more before it disappears and seeps into the ground-water channels where it makes its appearance in springs and wells. This was precisely the time at which the ecological panic button should have been hit, but apparently the warning that the naturalists, the fishermen, the hunters, and the ornithologists sounded seemed like the cry of "wolf!" to everyone else.

Foliage, through a process known as photosynthesis, removes impurities from the air, but the amount of foliage is continuously being diminished. At the same time more and more pollutants are being added to the relatively thin layer of the atmosphere. The plankton of the sea, which is being sentenced to death by pollution, manufactures three-quarters of our vital oxygen supply. In proportionate size, the belt of air around the earth can be compared with the peel on an orange.

Where there are atomic reactors there exists the terrible threat of human contact with radioactive material in cases of breakage or leakage.

The skin of the earth is being poisoned by the common use of inorganic nitrogen fertilizers. These chemicals, in turn, wash into the streams, lakes, and bays and seep into the ground water channels. This brings about a dense weeding, resulting in a deficiency of oxygen, in putrefaction, and in fish kills.

When there is no social consciousness of what constitutes permissible conduct, the result is aggression against nature, which in actuality is aggression against society. Not only do municipalities and industries pollute, but products—and their containers—do too, exhaust being a prime and critical example. The word "smog" made the headlines, and the word "dying" was applied to waters. But responsibility was neither assigned nor assumed. Fishermen, hunters, bird-watchers, and naturalists always observe and recognize environmental devastation first. This time the voice forecast the day of the gas mask and distilled water, but the outcry was unconvincing to others, who constitute the vast majority.

Things and people work in strange ways. Almost overnight a lady biologist accomplished what an army of anglers, hunters, conservation officials, ornithologists, naturalists and their organizations and their representatives had not been able to do.

Rachel Carson, in one fell swoop, convinced the American public that, as we continue to contaminate the environment, the existence of the human race is placed further in jeopardy. Her book reported rather than sermonized, and the message expressed in its title came through. *Silent Spring* fulfilled its destiny and became a best-seller.

"To everything there is a season and there is a time to every purpose." This was the time for the word "pollution" to become meaningful. From Sunday school to the poker table the state of the environment became a popular topic of conservation. Printed on the map of every mind was that dirty wood, pollution.

At first there was scattered private action, then action followed in quantity. Citizens groups, women's organizations, service clubs, voter's leagues, and political leaders were fascinated by the prospect of becoming leaders in the "new crusade." Not the least of the fledgling conservationists were located in the halls of ivy. Teachers and students alike conjured up such confounding questions as:

In the quest of his dream is it necessary that man foul his own nest?

What are the demands brought upon our resources and our ecology by each new birth?

Will we have to work ourselves to death to stay alive?

Do the decisions of nature command obedience?

Do we possess the technological means to escape from the environmental chaos which technology has incurred?

Could it be that mankind is involved in a race, the kind that is measured in time from start to finish? It might even be worse than that. Could this be the homestretch of the race, the finish being the end of mankind? There appears to be a parallel between man's fate and that of the extinct dodo.

Earlier in the century we first read about the Four Horsemen of the Apocalypse: War, Conquest, Famine, and Death. Today four horsemen ride again, The Four Horsemen of Ennui, and their names are Asphyxiation, Thirst, Poisoning, and Radiation. There appears to be no favorite; the race is that close.

When the last gasp has been taken by the last remaining

member of *Homo sapiens,* the creature endowed with a large brain and great mental capacity, will his extermination be because of polluted air, lack of oxygen, contaminated food from poisoned land, poisoned water from polluted ground water, or a degeneration of his organs caused by radioactive fallout?

"We have time, perhaps a generation, in which to save the environment from the final effect of the violence we have already done to it and save ourselves from our suicidal folly," states Dr. Barry Commoner, Director of the Center for the Biology of Natural Systems in St. Louis.

How accurate was Emerson when he wrote "Progress is the activity of today, and the assurance of tomorrow"? Certainly he appreciated the esthetic, and no doubt he regarded the best life as one varied in content. It is certain that to Emerson a vital American resource was the outdoors, its appreciation and its protection. Since his day a different pattern of time, space, and domination has developed. Were he living today there would be generated within him a profound skepticism of the old-fashioned idea of progress.

Havelock Ellis, the English scholar and physician, wrote: "The sun, the moon and the stars would have disappeared long ago had they been within reach of predatory human hands."

When that infamous Cleveland river was declared to be a fire hazard, people understood and they did not think it funny. A nation in disgust has read about, heard about, and talked about the oil blowouts off the California coast. Someone coined a new term—noise pollution. Sloppy people were given the name, "litter bugs." People asked what should be done with automobile graveyards.

An inspired writer once penned the following: "Where there is no vision, the people perish." (Proverbs 29:18.) The putrid circumstances stemming from an advanced technological system offer the younger generation, to whom time should be particularly kind and important, a golden opportunity to develop, support, and accomplish constructive ecological action. The enormity of the situation constitutes a challenge greater than that faced by any previous generation. Technology can be utilized to master the problems incurred by technology.

Such is the brief story of how the most plundered country on the planet has begun to mature. The important part of the story, however, remains to be written by a younger man—under the dateline January 1, 2000.

An angler attaches a lure to a line in the expectation of incurring a strike. It has been chosen because it can do a specific job and possesses a certain appeal. Many good lures have come and gone; many are available. For some situations, in order to have exactly what one wishes to cast to the fish, it is necessary to design and fabricate one's own; and there is abundant satisfaction in that.

The lures pictured in this book constitute the assortment, with much duplication eliminated, from which the author draws for his bass-muskie-pike escapades. Although not complete, it is representative of the various categories of the lure-making craft. Any not pictured will catch fish even as all such pictured have. This is a game of playing the percentages.

In the sport of casting, the expected comes so unexpectedly. That is the reason why in angling the strike of a game fish to a lure is so thrilling.

Index

Some Unobtainable "Greats"

Most of these lures are currently unavailable, but all are tremendous for their respective uses. It is not my purpose merely to describe how to make lures at home. Rather it is my hope that directions in this book for making certain unobtainable "greats" will make it possible for them to be placed in appreciative hands. (See chapter on HOMEMADE LURES, page 218.)

see front endleaf

Sick Sucker

The SICK SUCKER bobs and weaves on the surface under rod-tip persuasion, and with fast reeling it submerges and swims in a tantalizing manner comparable to other great lures. It has been tremendously effective on muskies, pike and chain pickerel in appropriate lure sizes.

FINISHES: Lure coloration catches both fish and fishermen. For the pike family, metallic paint, particularly hot copper and green, is highly effective. Bass seem to have a preference for white and yellow, but sometimes orange works best. Black is good at night. Purple and chartreuse are not used on SICK SUCKERS—but appear primarily in the plastic worm and grub field.

Assorted Lures

Top row, left to right: FLAT FISH type with pulling power; the Bates and Fox PAD JUMPER; the antique GAME FISHER, a jointed plug, in its two sizes; R.K. Rush's antique RUSH TANGO and a homemade MIDGE.

Bottom row: Five of Mack McGarrough's superb weighted bucktail and spinner lures called MINNO-BUGS; homemade SPOOK, a fine muskie casting lure; Robert's RIVER PUP, which is a baby MUD PUPPY; Garcia's ABOU-HI-LO (no longer available), the lure with the adjustable lip to regulate traveling depth; and Mepps' GIANT KILLER, a casting spoon for pike and muskies; an underwater lure to which has been added the Don DuBois patented spinner, which reverses direction every few seconds; and two homemade JERSEY WOWS made before Jim Donely sold the rights to Heddon, where it is known today as the CRAZY CRAWLER, a spattering surface lure.

FINISHES: (See pages 220-233 for specific information on each.) When super flash is desired, there is a new product to produce it on any lure. It is a prismatic and reflecting paste-on, convenient to apply and readily available. Small sheets are produced at Hood River, Oregon, by Luhr Jensen in both gold and silver base. Stick-on *Prism Lite* is gummed and backed by removable paper. It is cut to fit on the desired areas of the lure. Narrow strips are best because they do not buckle. After the paste-on, the lure can be coated with Epoxy glue, which not only secures the *Prism Lite* but also produces a hard, slippery finish.